GENIUS OF COMMON SENSE

JANE JACOBS and the story of

The Death and Life of Great American Cities

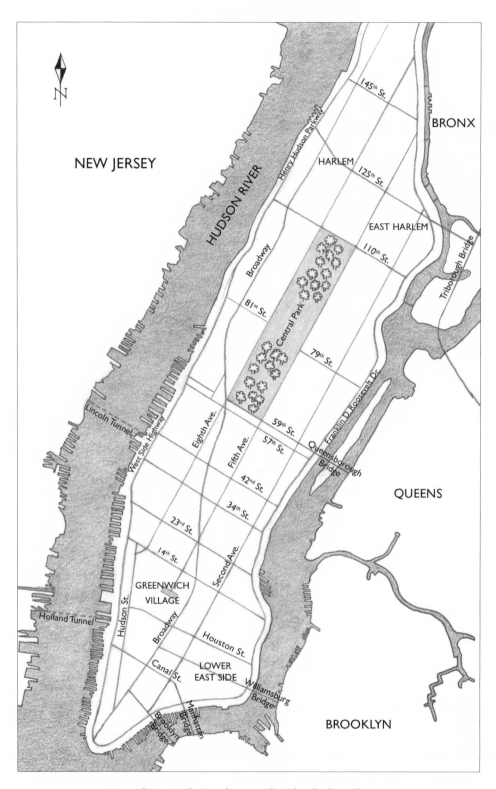

Map of New York City showing the island of Manhattan
between New Jersey and the westernmost parts of Long Island, Brooklyn and Queens

GLENNA LANG & MARJORY WUNSCH

GENIUS OF COMMON SENSE

JANE JACOBS and the story of

The Death and Life of Great American Cities

DAVID R. GODINE
Publisher
Boston

First published in 2009 by
David R. Godine · Publisher
Post Office Box 450
Jaffrey, New Hampshire 03452
www.godine.com

LIBRARY OF CONGRESS
CATALOGING-IN-PUBLICATION DATA
Lang, Glenna.
Genius of common sense : Jane Jacobs and the story of The
death and life of great American cities / by Glenna Lang &
Marjory Wunsch. — 1st ed.
p.   cm.
Includes bibliographical references and index.
ISBN 978-1-56792-384-1
1. Jacobs, Jane, 1916–2006—Juvenile literature.   2. Jacobs, Jane,
1916–2006. Death and life of great American cities—Juvenile
literature.   3. Women city planners—United States—Biography—
Juvenile literature.   4. City planners—United States—Biography
—Juvenile literature.   5. City planning—History—20th century—
Juvenile literature.   6. Sociology, Urban—History—20th century—
Juvenile literature.   7. City planning—New York (State)—
New York—History—20th century—Juvenile literature.
8. Neighborhood—New York (State)—New York—History—
20th century—Juvenile literature.   I. Wunsch, Marjory.   II. Title.
HT167.L319 2008
711'.4092—dc22
[B]
2009008304

FIRST PRINTING, 2009

Printed in Canada

For Alex and Esmé, with love . . . and squalor
– G.L.

For Nora, a city girl
– M.W.

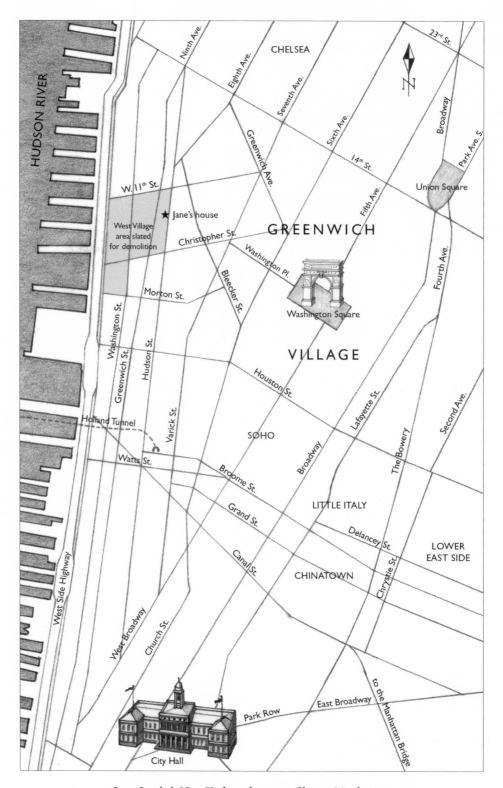

Jane Jacobs's New York, a close-up of lower Manhattan

CONTENTS

Obstreperous: noisily defiant; unruly; boisterous; unmanageable. [Latin *obstreperus,* from *obstrepere,* to make noise against]

– American Heritage Dictionary

CHAPTER ILLUSTRATIONS

* Illustration by Marjory Wunsch

** Illustration by Glenna Lang

CHAPTER ONE

An Obstreperous Young Girl

JANE ISABEL BUTZNER looked up from the book she was reading in her lap under her schoolroom desk. She heard her fourth-grade teacher explain that cities always develop around waterfalls. Jane thought about Scranton, the small northeastern Pennsylvania city where she lived in the 1920s, with its shallow winding river and hills all around. Most people worked in the nearby coal mines or in something related to the coal industry. Everybody knew that coal was what was most important in Scranton. Jane raised her hand, and her teacher nodded. Confidently, she told her teacher that it did not make sense that *all* cities grew up around waterfalls. Yes, she had seen a little waterfall in a park near her house, but it had nothing to do with Scranton or how the city came to be and prosper.

Jane's teacher sighed in exasperation at one more contradiction from this inquisitive and independent-minded student. Yet one day this sometimes obstreperous young girl would use her keen observations to write a world-changing book on American cities. Her book helped convince the government to stop bulldozing large areas of homes and thriving shops and encouraged people everywhere to appreciate the excitement and opportunities cities offered. Ultimately, Jane's book would help New York, Boston, and other cities to remain the vibrant places we treasure today. And Jane herself would participate in and lead battles to save the very neighborhoods she wrote about.

CHAPTER TWO

Growing Up in the Electric City

JANE WAS BORN into a family of free-thinking individuals from very different backgrounds. Her father, John Decker Butzner, a prominent and much-loved doctor, delivered the strapping baby girl to his wife, Bess Robison Butzner, on May 4, 1916. Jane was the third child born in their modest home on Electric Street in Scranton. Sadly, their second child, a boy, had died of a childhood illness. When Jane was born, her sister, Betty, was six. Their brother John arrived the next year and James a year and a half later.

Jane's mother, Bess Robison, belonged to a family with a tradition of working women. She grew up in a small town in the coal-mining country of Pennsylvania and had a career as a schoolteacher and a nurse in Philadelphia before she married. Her mother had also been a schoolteacher, and her aunt Hannah Breece taught on Indian reservations and in Alaskan villages.

Bess's father had served as a captain for the Union Army in the Civil War and told stories about being a captive at a Confederate prison in Virginia. He became a lawyer and ran for Congress in 1872 on the Greenback-Labor ticket, which Jane later described as a party whose ideas – like switching to paper money – seemed "outlandish" at the time but were eventually accepted. Other Robison ancestors had arrived in the colonies before the American Revolution.

Generations of the Butzner side of Jane's family, however, came from Virginia, a Confederate and pro-slavery state during the Civil War. But many

Butzners had opposed slavery, secession from the Union, and their state's participation in the Civil War. Jane's father, Decker, as he was called, was proud of these family members for asserting an unpopular point of view. He grew up on

Jane's father, John Decker Butzner, was a family physician.

Jane's mother, Bess Robison Butzner, worked as a nurse and teacher.

a farm near Fredericksburg in a family without much money and attended a one-room school where a young woman from the extended family taught the many cousins. Thanks to a rich uncle, Decker and his cousins went to college. Decker attended the University of Virginia and earned his medical degree.

Jane's mother and father met at a hospital in Philadelphia where Decker Butzner was finishing his medical training and Bess Robison worked as the supervising night nurse. They married and moved to Scranton in 1905, where Dr. Butzner began his career as a family physician.

Having grown up in rural areas, Decker and Bess Butzner thought cities were superior places to live. Their new hometown of Scranton was the flourishing capital of Lackawanna County and the seventh most populous city in

Pennsylvania. With theaters, a museum, and a public library among its many architecturally splendid buildings, it was the largest city in a patchwork quilt of anthracite-coal mining towns. Scranton's early settlers had discovered large deposits of this highest-quality, hard coal that yields great heat with little flame or smoke. Anthracite had fueled Scranton's iron furnaces and now powered its railroads and its factories, whose products ranged from rails to silk. Italian, Polish, and Russian immigrants joined the earlier wave of Germans, Irish, and Welsh to work in the mines and factories, creating a rich cultural mix.

Scranton supplied coal to the nation at a time when power plants, factories, transportation, and homes all ran on coal. One could even see collieries, which processed coal above the mines, within the city limits. From the grand Lackawanna Station, trains carried freight and passengers to other parts of the country. Scranton's dense downtown bustled with shoppers scurrying to department stores and businessmen dashing to banks and tall office buildings.

Wyoming Avenue in downtown Scranton with domed Coal Exchange Building on right, 1930s. Jane rode a streetcar on the Dunmore line (shown here) to and from school.

Jane with her younger brothers,
Jim (middle) and John (right).

The Butzners lived in a residential section on the edge of Scranton. When Jane was four, her family moved to the adjacent borough of Dunmore and into a fine brick house, the largest on the block. She attended the George Washington School #3, only a few blocks away in her Dunmore neighborhood. People often commented that Jane looked like her father. She had straw-yellow hair, bright blue eyes, a distinctive nose, and was tall for her age. One of her classmates called Jane "a free spirit, clever, hilariously funny and fearless." Much to the dismay of the teachers, she amused herself and her friends with endless mischievous pranks. In the grade-school lunchroom she blew up paper bags and exploded them loudly. In her less flamboyant moments she read voraciously on all sorts of topics and loved to ride her bike.

Jane was close to her father and had great respect for him and his ideas. He taught her to look up subjects in the encyclopedia and encouraged all his children to think for themselves. One day when Jane was seven, Dr. Butzner explained the seriousness of promises. One should never make a promise one could not keep. Especially as a child, one should never promise to do something for the rest of his or her life. So when Jane's third-grade teacher asked the class to raise their hands if they promised to brush their teeth every day for the rest of their lives, Jane refused to raise her hand and urged the other children not to raise theirs. She explained her father's reasoning, but this hardly calmed her infuriated teacher. Jane was expelled from school for the day, but she returned as confident as ever. "It gave me the feeling I was independent," she recalled.

While still in elementary school, Jane began writing poetry. She sent some of her poems to a family friend, Thomas Lomax Hunter, who wrote a column in the Fredericksburg, Virginia, newspaper. Delighted with the eleven-year-old's work, he published Jane's poem called "The Flapper," a term for a 1920s fashionable young woman of rebellious style and attitude. Hunter expressed

Jane's childhood home, now 1712 (formerly 1728) Monroe Avenue, Dunmore, in 2007. The mainly residential, adjacent borough of Dunmore serves as an extension of Scranton.

New York harbor and skyline with the Hudson River on the left and the East River on right, 1925, as it looked on Jane's first visit.

his enthusiasm and encouragement to Jane in a letter: "I know that a person with such talent will cultivate it. Some day you will be a poetess of distinction."

Dr. Butzner had a downtown office and was one of the first doctors in town to have a car. In his little red Ford with no windshield or roof, he drove to tend his patients in their own homes, often far away. But to go downtown, the Butzner family took the streetcar, which ran on tracks and was powered by electricity. In the 1880s Scranton opened the first successful electric street-car system in the United States and was one of the first cities to use electric street lights, giving the city its nickname still used today, "The Electric City."

Like many children in her neighborhood, starting in eighth grade Jane went to school in downtown Scranton. Perhaps her favorite part of school was getting there on the streetcar "painted fuchsia or silver or sky blue" with "flowered chintz seat covers." She felt her life enlarge with the excitement of the lively streets and the variety of stores that downtown offered.

When Jane was twelve, she welcomed the chance to visit another city, the largest in the United States. With a friend's family, she traveled to New

Looking north on Fifth Avenue near 48th Street, New York City, 1930.
Note the flapper woman on the left in dark coat and pointy shoes.

York for the first time in her life. They drove one hundred twenty miles – a long trip in those days – to a town in New Jersey on the wide mouth of the Hudson River. Here they left their car to board a ferry, arriving at one of the many piers that ringed the island of Manhattan. They had entered one of the world's largest centers of trade, the booming port of New York. Along the waterfront, longshoremen unloaded large freighters, and passengers disembarked from majestic ocean liners.

However exciting Scranton appeared, New York City far surpassed it during the prosperous era of the Roaring Twenties. The sight of the city, with its skyscrapers and elevated trains, made a lasting impression on Jane. "I was flabbergasted at all the people in the streets. It was lunchtime in Wall

ABOVE: Jane's diploma from Central High School in downtown Scranton. The engraving depicts the striking building still in use today.

RIGHT: Jane's high school graduation photo, 1933.

Street in 1928 and . . . the city was just jumping. It was all full of people," she recollected. Near the New York Stock Exchange on Wall Street, wealthy businessmen and fashionably dressed people thronged the streets. On Fifth Avenue, flapper women, whom Jane had imagined in her poem, paraded their low-waisted dresses and bobbed hair. The number of cars, trucks, and double-decker buses caused traffic jams everywhere.

Jane saw New York in all its glory. The following year, the stock market crashed. Many investors lost their fortunes, companies closed, and workers lost their jobs. The era known as the Great Depression began. People all over the country were plunged into poverty. Scrantonians were already experiencing hard times because Scranton's mines and businesses had begun closing ten years earlier. Now with the Depression the economic situation worsened, and many of Dr. Butzner's patients could not afford to pay him for his services.

In high school Jane continued writing poetry and also continued her pranks. "The peak of her shenanigans" took place in a downtown department store during the school's lunch break. Jane charged up the narrow and crowded down-escalator. One of her "giggling friends" later remembered: "The store floor walker, looking wrathful, was waiting for her at the top."

Much to the relief of her parents, the rebellious Jane graduated from Scranton's Central High School in January 1933. She had received a "classical" or general education, after which many graduates headed off to work. Although her parents offered to pay for college, Jane chose not to go because she was "thoroughly sick of . . . school and eager to get a job, writing or reporting." But Jane's parents thought their children should learn a practical skill to help them find a job, in addition to pursuing their most desired careers. So Jane studied stenography, a kind of shorthand note-taking before the use of tape recorders, at the Powell School of Business. She completed the secretarial course that June and became, in her own opinion, "a good stenographer."

Seventeen years old and still at home, Jane followed her passion and found her first job. As an unpaid assistant to the women's-page editor at the *Scranton Tribune*, she reported on such ordinary events as church suppers, weddings, parties, and club meetings. Occasionally she could choose and write stories that interested her. After a year at the newspaper, Jane's parents suggested she visit her aunt Martha Robison and see a much different part of the country. Martha ran a community center in Higgins, North Carolina, "a bypassed pocket of the Appalachian Mountains." Jane later reflected on how outsiders like her aunt had helped these talented but poor people "regain lost skills" – such as making rag rugs and handwoven linens – and take an "interest in the future and its opportunities."

But after six months in Appalachia with her aunt, Jane felt the lure of the big city and the desire to seek her fortune.

CHAPTER THREE

Becoming a Writer in New York

WITH A TASTE for new experiences, Jane, now eighteen years old, set out for New York City in 1934 to pursue her career as a writer. New York had changed dramatically since her previous visit. "I could see contrasts, even from that first visit. Especially downtown. There were a lot more unemployed people in '34 and there weren't any in '28," she said. The Great Depression had struck the city. With so many bankrupt businesses, people were having a hard time finding work. If they found jobs, these often paid lower wages than what they had earned previously. Or the company would go out of business, and the search for a job began again.

Jane's sister, Betty, had already moved to New York. Betty had studied to be an interior designer in Philadelphia but could not find a position in that field. Instead she worked as a salesgirl in a department store in Brooklyn. Betty rented an apartment with enough room for her younger sister, so Jane moved in. It was on the top floor of a six-story building with no elevator in Brooklyn Heights, across the river from more bustling Manhattan. After paying the rent, there was little money left over, so the sisters sometimes could afford to eat only Pablum, an inexpensive soft baby cereal.

Every morning Jane scoured the want ads for writing jobs or any other kind of work. With a lead for a possible job, she walked across the Brooklyn Bridge into Manhattan. She loved the city, "a complicated, great place."

The Brooklyn Bridge walkway into Manhattan, c. 1900,
was Jane's route into Manhattan, too.

After she was turned down for a job, she spent the afternoon exploring
whatever neighborhood she found herself in. If she had already seen that
neighborhood, she took the subway somewhere else. One day, just because
she liked the name, she got off at the Christopher Street subway stop. "I was
enchanted with this neighborhood," Jane reflected. She walked around the
area all afternoon and then told Betty, "I found out where we have to live."

Jane had discovered Greenwich Village with its charming buildings and
angled streets. An intriguing mixture of ethnic groups and a variety of workers peopled the neighborhood, with shopkeepers, laborers, writers, and artists
side by side. Shoe repairs and fish, meat, and produce markets nestled

between book stores, cafes, theaters, and music clubs. For decades the Village had attracted an artistic population and was known as the city's center of creativity.

Jane's skill as a stenographer came in handy, and she landed a job as a secretary, earning $12 a week at a candy manufacturing company. She and Betty could now afford to move to Morton Street in Greenwich Village, where Jane kept on writing. Within months, the *New York Herald Tribune,* one of the city's great newspapers, published her poem "While Arranging Verses for a Book" about the art of writing and how she struggled to find "the perfect word to clothe the perfect thought."

For five years, while Jane worked as a secretary at a series of small companies, she also investigated the city. In between jobs as she looked for work, she wandered through Manhattan's exciting fur, flower, leather, and diamond districts, where these products were bought and sold in large quantities. On the street she stopped to ask shopkeepers and workers about their business, and took notes on scraps of paper in her purse. Using her talent for poetic

Entrance to Jane's apartment building at 55 Morton Street, Greenwich Village, a six-story building with an elevator on a curving, tree-lined street.

description, she turned her observations about these working neighborhoods into vivid articles. She decided to submit her pieces on each of these industries to the fashion magazine *Vogue,* which accepted several of her articles for the startling sum of $40 each – almost a month's salary. The *Herald Tribune* published some of her feature stories as well, although they paid less handsomely.

After the thrill of earning part of her living from published articles, Jane

Old manhole covers from Greenwich Village, 2007,
the subject of Jane's article, "Caution · Men Working: Read the monograms on manholes and you will know what runs underneath."

suffered a tragic blow. Her beloved father had fallen ill. She and her brothers and sister returned to Scranton to gather at Decker Butzner's hospital bedside. Jane's father, who had been a great inspiration to her, died in 1937 at the age of fifty-nine. The entire community mourned his loss. The local newspaper praised him for dedicating his life to the "alleviation of suffering."

Jane returned to New York with a heavy heart, but surely felt comforted by thinking of how her scientifically minded and thoughtful father had encouraged her to observe and think for herself. As she walked around the city that fascinated her, she noticed the hundreds of metal manhole covers, what she called "the lowly iron waffles," embedded in the city streets. "The lights of New York are the city's jewels, but her buttons and hooks and eyes are the squares and circles of metal that dot the asphalt and sidewalks," she began her 1940 article in *Cue* magazine. By reading the letters on the manhole covers, she discovered that you could tell what was running below. Likening herself to a scientific observer, a "city naturalist," Jane followed the trail of "underground spaghetti." She traced the rivers, steam, gas, and electricity, and even "five hundred letters in a pneumatic [air-powered] tube,

Ruggiero's Fish Market, 235 Bleecker Street, Greenwich Village,
a typical commercial block not far from Christopher Street, in the 1960s.

Hazan Locksmith, 131 Rivington Street, Lower East Side, 1960s, an interesting neighborhood to explain to imaginary conversation partners.

clipping along at thirty miles an hour on their way to an uptown post office."

Jane developed a unique method to understand the world around her. Ever since childhood, she imagined having conversations with people from an earlier time in history and describing what she saw to someone completely unfamiliar with the modern age. She had started with Thomas Jefferson but grew bored with him because he seemed most interested in abstract ideas. Ben Franklin, in contrast, asked good down-to-earth questions. "He's rather shocked with the way women are dressed," she commented, "but he gets used to it." Her conversations explored such things as how the traffic lights worked. A medieval Saxon named Cerdic proved most useful because almost everything had to be explained to him.

At twenty-two, with her career as a writer underway, Jane decided to explore some of her many interests by taking college classes. Since she worked as a secretary by day, she took classes at the University Extension at Columbia University in the evenings. Jane could not officially *attend* Columbia because it only admitted men, but the University Extension allowed anyone to enroll in classes alongside regular Columbia students – a perfect solution for someone who had a strong desire for learning, but who wanted to set her own terms. There was no fixed program of study, so Jane could choose whatever courses appealed to her. Pursuing her love of science, she studied geology first, then chemistry and embryology, moving on to zoology, law, political science, and economics. The classes fascinated her, and she worked hard. For the first time, this formerly difficult student received good grades.

Jane's enthusiasm for the course she took on Constitutional law led her to research the records of the Constitutional Convention, where the Founding

Students in front of Low Library on Columbia University's campus, 1940s. For two years Jane took classes at the University Extension, her only formal exposure to higher education.

Fathers had hashed out their conflicting points of view. With her zest for a topic she found riveting, Jane compiled an entire book of the rejected proposals of the writers of the Constitution, contrasting the constitution we have with "constitutions we might have had." In 1941, when Jane was only twenty-five, Columbia University Press published her book, *Constitutional Chaff:*

The Diamond Mine and Colliery, named for the hardness of anthracite coal, was the oldest colliery in Scranton. It opened in 1852 and operated until 1933.

Rejected Suggestions of the Constitutional Convention of 1787, with Explanatory Argument. An eminent reviewer hailed her scholarly contribution.

After two years of taking classes, Jane began work at *The Iron Age* magazine, where she wrote articles about the metals industry. The U.S. joined the Allies and entered World War II after the bombing of Pearl Harbor on December 7, 1941. During the war, manufacturers in the defense industry needed up-to-date information as factories turned out planes, ships, and tanks for the military. Jane wrote about new materials and products for this wartime equipment and also covered the economic effects of the war.

The campaign to save Scranton, a flier displaying:
A=Jane's 1943 article in *Iron Age*, B=Newspapers that picked up the story,
C=Thank-you letter to *Iron Age* from Scranton advocate E.M. Elliott.

In March 1943, Jane used one of her *Iron Age* features to call attention to
the dire situation in her hometown of Scranton. In the early 1940s, 25,000
coal miners had lost their jobs when the anthracite in some of the collieries
was exhausted. More than 7,000 houses stood empty as people left to search
for work elsewhere. In her article Jane worried that her city would become a
ghost town. Why, she asked, weren't more companies locating in Scranton,

an ideal place to manufacture goods for the armed forces? There was ample transportation, plentiful fuel, and skilled people eager for work.

Several hundred newspapers nationwide picked up Jane's story, "Scranton, Neglected City." People read the story in Chicago, Baltimore, Seattle, Boston, Philadelphia, and Kansas City. Jane published another article about Scranton's plight in the *New York Herald Tribune* and participated in a letter-

Murray Corporation of America's B-29 bomber wing factory, which opened in Scranton in December 1943.

writing campaign that targeted federal and state officials, pointing out the advantages of Scranton for new industries. As a principal speaker at a protest rally in her hometown, she called upon the government to use the region's many resources by opening factories there. Led by the *Scranton Tribune*, local civic organizations also campaigned vigorously for more industry.

These combined efforts paid off, and new factories began to open. "Net results so far during the past month," E. M. Elliott, Scranton's representative in Washington, wrote to *Iron Age* in April 1943, "a bag factory, a clothing manufacturing plant, two plants to make metal products, and the Murray Corp. of America is to build a 500,000 sq. ft. plant, to employ 7,000 persons." A headline in the *Scrantonian* proudly proclaimed: "Ex-Scranton Girl Helps Home City: Miss Butzner's Story in Iron Age Brought Nationwide Publicity." Jane had become a writer whose words not only informed people but could also move them to act.

Despite her outstanding work for *Iron Age*, the magazine regarded Jane as a troublemaker. Her boss, who had a low regard for women, referred to her as a "mere typist" even though she had been promoted to associate editor and was writing important articles.

The company that owned *Iron Age* also thought of Jane as trouble. They had threatened to fire workers who belonged to a labor union, and some members of the magazine had joined a labor union to ask for fairer pay. People in clerical jobs were paid much too little, and a woman editor earned half the salary of a man doing the same job.

Jane could not tolerate these injustices. She became a union representative and helped make sure that company officials allowed workers to make their demands without fear of retaliation. Jane put her childhood obstreperousness to good use: she began standing up not only for herself but for others as well.

CHAPTER FOUR

Cupid and the Candy-Store House

Later in 1943, Jane moved on to a new job as a writer at the U.S. government's Office of War Information, which aimed to inspire patriotism and convince Americans to aid the war effort. When the Second World War ended and the office closed in 1945, Jane went to work for another part of the federal government, the State Department's Magazine Branch. Writing features for a glossy magazine with beautiful photographs called *Amerika Illustrated*, Jane helped to celebrate American democracy in contrast to life under communist dictatorships. These pieces were then translated into Russian so people in the communist-ruled Soviet Union could learn about the United States.

Amerika had articles on such topics as Texas farmers and the medical uses of atomic energy – even a piece on air-conditioning, which was then unknown in the Soviet Union. Her new position gave Jane the chance to explore and write about subjects that would continue to interest her – building in America, school planning, reconstruction of rundown neighborhoods, housing for people without much money, and life in American cities such as Philadelphia and Washington, D.C.

One evening in March 1944 during her time at the Office of War Information, Jane and her sister threw a party in their Greenwich Village apartment. Robert Hyde Jacobs Jr., a young, dark-haired architect working as an

Page from Jane's article in *Amerika Illustrated* magazine No. 43, 1950, on "Planned Reconstruction of Lagging City Areas." The Russian caption describes the benefits of these affordable apartments built in New York.

aircraft designer, was among the guests that Betty invited. "It was as if Cupid had shot that arrow," Jane mused later. She and Bob fell in love almost instantly. They were married in May and would have married sooner, but they held off so that she could meet Bob's parents.

The small, informal wedding took place at the Butzners' home in Scranton with only family members present. True to her nonconformist nature, the twenty-eight-year-old bride wore "a street-length dress trimmed with turquoise and fuchsia." Afterwards the newlyweds set off for their version of the

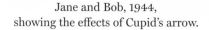
Jane and Bob, 1944,
showing the effects of Cupid's arrow.

Jane and Bob's wedding photo, May 1944,
Scranton, Pennsylvania.

ideal honeymoon – a bicycle trip through northern Pennsylvania and upstate New York. This was the start of a long and happy marriage. Jane would fondly describe her supportive husband as her "coach and cheerleader."

Bob and Jane Jacobs, as she now called herself, lived for a while in Jane's apartment off Washington Square, the lovely park in the center of the Village where people walked dogs, played music, or relaxed on benches in the shade. In 1947, wishing for a home of their own, they bought an old three-story, six-room, brick-faced building at 555 Hudson Street, with a candy-store at street level, in a rough and somewhat industrial section of West Greenwich Village. With Bob's skills as an architect, they gradually fixed it up, doing much of the work themselves. They replaced the front wall, which was collapsing, and all its windows and made the back wall on the ground floor entirely glass, looking out over the rather bare backyard.

Bob, Jane, and their son Jimmy in front of the "candy-store house"
at 555 Hudson Street before major renovation of the façade.

"The house was pretty primitive in those days with no central heating," recollected a friend.

The Jacobses' "candy-store house" was set snugly between a laundry and
a tailor shop. From the rear windows they could watch a sculptor neighbor
carving a figure in white stone when he wasn't working at Macy's department store. The kitchen and front bedrooms faced Hudson Street, a busy
thoroughfare lined with stores, eating places, and other businesses.

To most people Hudson Street appeared to be a "clutter of traffic between
two lines of warehouses, factories, shops, bars, churches, and elderly apartment houses." But to Jane and Bob their West Village neighborhood, like
other city neighborhoods, was a "wonderful place for children to grow up"
because it was "densely populated and complicated and interesting . . . filled
with people with different backgrounds, jobs, and nationalities." Everyone
lived in apartments above the shops or in buildings interspersed with small
businesses and light industry.

In 1948 their first child, James Kedzie Jacobs (usually called Jimmy),
was born. Two years later his brother, Edward Decker Jacobs (almost always

called Ned), came along. With a full-time writing job and two young children, Jane was now a busy working mother.

Motherhood gave Jane another perspective on the city. Awakened to tend a baby in the early morning hours, she often sat in the dark and peered out her window on Hudson Street. She liked "seeing the shadows and hearing the sounds of the sidewalk." Her curiosity was always at work. What was it, she wondered, that kept her neighborhood a safe and lively place?

Jane's large ideas grew from many small observations. She listened to "snatches of party conversation" or sometimes to singing or even crying at three o'clock in the morning. One winter night, she saw a bagpiper, who seemed to appear out of nowhere, attract a crowd. Some people on the sidewalk below began to dance the Highland Fling. Others watched from their windows and applauded. Jane saw that, night and day, the street was safe because it was always in use. To her, these comings and goings appeared as "an intricate sidewalk ballet."

Later in the morning when Jane put out her garbage can, she watched

Hudson Street morning sidewalk ballet with girl on scooter and delivery man, 2008. Jane's block and the "candy-store house" (now a children's clothing store) with tree in front.

the ballet begin as "droves of junior high school students walk[ed] by the center of the stage dropping candy wrappers." Owners of nearby businesses – the laundry, delicatessen, barber, and hardware store – would open for the day. Young children soon filled the sidewalk as they headed for nearby elementary schools. Men and women, like Jane, thronged the streets on their way to work.

On her days off, Jane observed the "heart-of-the-day" ballet when workers on their lunch break crowded into a neighborhood restaurant, coffeehouse, or bakery lunchroom. Later, mothers with baby carriages came out, and, after school, teenagers did their homework on their stoops, sitting on the steps leading up to their front doors.

Jane also noticed what she called the "character dancers," people like "a strange old man with strings of old shoes over his shoulders" and "motor-scooter riders with big beards." The ballet reached its climax late in the afternoon as the street filled with children on tricycles, roller skates, and stilts. As evening came and stores closed up, pizza shops and

People lingering, dancing, playing music, young and old, . . .

bars enlivened the scene. The fascinating dance of the city never stopped.

Through her window or during her walks, Jane watched constantly and mulled things over in her own way. She took into account her observations of the city life around her when she wrote articles at work or on her own to submit to magazines. One day these observations would form the basis of an influential book that would change the way many people thought about what made cities lively and livable.

in a contemporary sidewalk ballet, Washington Square, 2007.

CHAPTER FIVE

Reporting and Learning at *Architectural Forum*

IN 1952 the Magazine Branch of the State Department closed its New York office, and once again Jane looked for work. Fascinated by science, she considered taking a job with *Natural History* magazine. But she chose instead to try a position at the country's most respected magazine about architecture, *Architectural Forum*. Jane had no experience as an architect, but the magazine's editor thought this might be all to the good. Perhaps she could look at buildings with a fresh eye.

Jane had to learn quickly, for her editor asked her to cover the architecture of hospitals and schools. Her architect husband, Bob, taught her how to read the technical drawings that architects prepare for contractors, showing how to put a building's parts together. Before long Jane was writing about all kinds of buildings, not just schools and hospitals. She also reported on city planning – the arrangement of different components of the city such as streets, buildings, and parks. Planners gave advice on which areas should have homes, stores, schools, or factories and where to build roads. During her ten years at the magazine, Jane would write articles for almost every one of their monthly issues and edit many others.

Jane arrived at *Architectural Forum* at a crucial time for America's big cities. All across the country, city leaders – mayors, downtown bankers, owners of big department stores – and city planners worried about their

Jane in her office at *Architectural Forum*,
the premier magazine for discussing urban issues.

cities. Few downtown office buildings had been built since the Depression, and with more income to buy automobiles, wealthy and even middle-class families were choosing to live in the suburbs instead of the city. These families often associated crime, poverty, and disease with city neighborhoods and were lured by the attractions of a suburban single-family house and a yard. If too many middle-class people left, the urban leaders feared that the nation's great cities, and especially their downtowns, would wither and die.

Just as worrisome to the city leaders were the changes to the neighborhoods. Since the Second World War, working-class people – African Americans and Appalachians from the South, Puerto Ricans and Mexicans – had been streaming into cities to find jobs. The newcomers did not earn much money, and the formerly middle-class neighborhoods into which they moved began to look shabby. Even worse, racial discrimination kept African Americans and other nonwhites confined to certain parts of the city and forced many people to crowd together in small apartments. Some landlords took advantage of the situation and allowed their buildings to become

Urban blight, inside and out:
Backyard slum somewhere in Manhattan (left) and
a foot coming through the ceiling of an apartment in need of repair in East Harlem (right).

dangerous slums, overcrowded, in disrepair, and unfit for people to live in.

Urban planners thought of the deterioration of these neighborhoods as a kind of blight that, like a disease on a plant, could spread and kill the city. Planners and officials called for fixing the blighted neighborhoods by knocking down whole blocks of old buildings and replacing them with gleaming new structures – a concept known as urban renewal. Sometimes in place of the old buildings, developers built luxury housing, government centers, or theaters. Other times they hoped to rescue low-income people from unsafe and congested houses by building new homes for them, "public housing" funded and managed by the government. The money for tearing down

Urban renewal replaced Boston's thriving West End with this high-rise housing development of luxury apartments called Charles River Park, c. 1960.

districts regarded as slums and then rebuilding them came from the federal government by means of a law called the Housing Act of 1949.

The modern style of sleek, tall buildings represented a new and better way of life. With the hard times of the Depression and the Second World War behind them, Americans hungered for new houses, modern appliances, and the latest-model cars. So when leaders tried to find cures for urban blight, they envisioned new buildings in the modern style.

From their offices at Rockefeller Center, the editors at *Architectural Forum* looked out over midtown Manhattan. They wanted to make their magazine the foremost place to discuss modern architecture and debate the difficult issues facing the city. In their pages, they tried to answer pressing questions: What was the best way to pursue urban renewal and rebuild America's cities? Should people live in high-rise or low-rise buildings? How should urban spaces be organized to make room for the automobile? Where should businesses and homes be located in relation to one another?

Jane's travels to research material for *Architectural Forum* – and one fortunate meeting – helped shape her thinking about these topics. In 1954

The lively street life of the North End, Boston, 1950s.
This neighborhood was adjacent and similar to Boston's demolished West End.

Edmund Bacon, a well-known city planner, took Jane on a tour of Philadelphia. The tour began with a walk along a crowded street in a poor neighborhood. It was a lively scene. "People were looking out of their windows," Jane observed, or sitting on stoops, and "kids [were] playing in the street." Bacon proudly showed Jane a new high-rise public housing project one street away. Looking around, she sensed that something was not right. While the people on the messy crowded street seemed to be "enjoying themselves and each other," Jane saw that the tidy streets of the new project were empty, "except for a little boy kicking a tire." Perhaps Edmund Bacon ("the big pooh-bah" as she later referred to him) had gotten it wrong. Perhaps the schemes that looked so good to the architects and planners were not really working.

Jane later traveled to Boston, where she saw a parallel situation. There she admired the North End neighborhood with its compact array of bakeries, shoe stores, and other small shops among low-rise apartments. People of all ages hung out on the streets. Convinced of the benefits of urban renewal, the city government had torn down an entire neighborhood – the adjacent and similar West End – and built sterile high-rises on the bulldozed land.

In 1955, Jane left her job briefly for a welcome interruption, the birth of her daughter, Mary (who later chose the name Burgin, her paternal grandmother's maiden name). In just a few weeks, she returned to work, as she had after the births of Jimmy and Ned. Jane and Bob hired a babysitter to care for the baby and her brothers during the day.

Back at *Architectural Forum*, Jane continued to wonder about the wisdom of large urban renewal projects in cities like New York, Boston, and Philadelphia. Then, one day, she met someone who shared her doubts.

William Kirk, an Episcopal minister, had come to the magazine's offices to visit a friend who was an editor there. Kirk was head of the Union Settlement, an organization that provided aid to poor people in the upper Manhattan neighborhood of East Harlem. Offering programs in areas such as education, nutrition, and recreation, the Settlement served growing numbers of Puerto Ricans and African Americans. Kirk, who had worked in East Harlem since 1949, was able to see what happened when aging neighbor-

William Kirk, in his office at the Union Settlement in East Harlem, showed Jane "a way of seeing" neighborhoods and downtowns.

Grant Houses in Harlem, super-blocks of a public housing project completed in 1957 by the New York City Housing Authority.

hoods were destroyed and replaced by large high-rise public housing projects. He and Jane soon became friends.

Kirk invited Jane to tour East Harlem with him. He showed her how widespread demolition had severed valuable social networks. Enormous "super-blocks" of tower housing lacked places like newsstands and corner stores that brought people together. From high-rise buildings, parents could not watch their children playing outside. As crime increased, people feared using the elevators, and children stayed away from the playgrounds. Despite the millions of dollars the U.S. government had spent to improve East Harlem, poverty, crime, and living conditions were *not* improving – they were getting worse. The neighborhood was *less* safe, its inhabitants *less* satisfied.

Jane was deeply troubled by the problems Kirk and his co-workers were trying to solve. Somehow she found the time to join the Union Settlement Board and help William Kirk draw the attention of city officials to East Harlem's situation. One of her major accomplishments was making it possible for East Harlem residents to become involved with the design of public housing in their neighborhood. Being a skilled writer was not enough for Jane. She became actively involved with the issues she cared about.

CHAPTER SIX

Jane's Good *Fortune* Article

IN 1956 Jane had an opportunity that, unbeknownst to her, would change her life. When her editor at *Architectural Forum* was unable to give a speech at Harvard University, he asked Jane to go in his place. At first she was reluctant to speak because she suffered from severe stage fright all her life. Surprisingly, the former class cut-up who popped bags in the school cafeteria felt timid when she had to talk in front of a large audience. But Jane finally accepted – on the condition that she could say whatever she wanted. And she memorized her ten-minute speech to ensure that she would get through the ordeal of speaking publicly.

Jane gave a star performance. Her straight talk stirred up the audience as she attacked the misguided efforts of city planners who favored the dull super-blocks of high-rise housing over smaller-scale buildings along city streets. She argued that without little places like candy stores and diners, there would be fewer and fewer places for people to meet. In one East Harlem project, Jane noted, the laundry was the only area that served as a social center for adults! The bulldozing of homes, businesses, storefront churches, and political clubs had destroyed whole communities. Urban renewal was hurting the very people it was intended to help.

William Whyte, an editor at *Fortune* – a popular and influential business magazine with a large general readership – was in the audience. Impressed by Jane's original ideas, he asked her to write an article for *Fortune*'s forth-coming series on cities called "The Exploding Metropolis." Others who worked for the magazine "had their doubts" about "a woman – especially one who rode her bicycle to work, spent her free time as a neighborhood activist,

Jane riding home from work on her bicycle, Washington Street, 1963.
The bicycle was Jane's preferred mode of transportation.

and," they claimed, "had never written a major article." But William Whyte prevailed, and Jane was on her way to becoming a public figure.

"You've got to get out and walk," Jane declared in her widely read *Fortune* article called "Downtown Is for People." She urged her readers to notice what made cities fun. And, as in her Harvard speech, she called for ways of building that would promote the "cheerful hurly-burly" of street life.

"This is a critical time for the future of the city," Jane wrote. "All over the country civic leaders and planners are preparing . . . redevelopment projects that will set the character of the center of our cities for generations to come."

"What will the projects look like?" she asked. Then, mocking the "experts," Jane answered her own question. "They will be spacious, parklike, and uncrowded. They will feature long green vistas. They will be stable and symmetrical and orderly. They will be clean, impressive, and monumental. They will have all the attributes of a well-kept, dignified cemetery."

While Jane agreed that many downtowns had become dirty, congested places, she railed once more against rebuilding with large-scale projects that would "banish the street." She praised successful urban spaces such as

Arlington Street, Boston. The church, a beloved landmark, creates a focal point on the corner of Boylston Street, a major thoroughfare.

Maiden Lane in San Francisco and Rockefeller Center in New York, where variations in the streetscape made urban life "surprising and delightful."

Stressing the value of focal points like fountains, clocks, squares, or unusual buildings, Jane admired places like Times Square in Manhattan, with its dazzling array of signs, and Arlington Street in Boston, where a

Times Square at night, with its brightly lit signs, 2007.
Located near the theater district, it is just as bustling during the day.

church steeple punctuates a row of buildings like an exclamation point. She wrote that our sense of being in a particular urban space "is built up . . . from many little things . . . some so small people take them for granted," such as "different kinds of paving, signs and fireplugs and street lights, white marble stoops." She challenged planners to take advantage of features that made one city unlike any other. Could a city built on hills offer interesting changes in level? Was there a waterfront that could be more fully enjoyed? Every great city, she thought, should treasure its individuality.

Jane went on to introduce the idea of the "two-shift city." To illustrate her concept, she pointed to New York's Fifty-seventh Street with its famous concert space, Carnegie Hall. On this block, Jane noted, a rich mixture of residences, theaters, restaurants, and small offices assured that pedestrians were on the street both day and night, using the street continuously. Jane roused her readers to consider odd questions, such as, "Why is a good steak house usually in an old building?" or "Why are short blocks apt to be busier than long ones?"

Carnegie Hall during the day, 2007.
At night concert-goers throng the same street.

Before long, Jane would have many more readers turning their thinking about American cities upside-down. People at the Rockefeller Foundation, an organization that supported leading research in urban design, had learned of Jane's work and understood its importance. They wanted her to expand the ideas she had set forth in her *Fortune* article, so they awarded her a grant. The grant provided Jane enough money to take time off from her job at *Architectural Forum* and devote all her time to writing a book on cities. Still another honor followed. Jason Epstein, an editor at Random House, a prestigious New York publisher, eagerly offered to publish Jane's book. This was the beginning of a long working relationship, for he was to remain her editor for most of her life. Jane appreciated Epstein's talents as a perceptive and open-minded editor who made good suggestions without changing what she had to say or her unique way of saying it.

CHAPTER SEVEN

A Bunch of Mothers . . . and Children

WHILE JANE WAS writing her book about urban planning and cities, something happened that pulled her away from her work. From her neighborhood network of friends, she learned of a scheme to run a four-lane highway right through nearby Washington Square Park. With its magnificent marble arch and a fountain in the center, Washington Square had long been the heart of Greenwich Village. Now a powerful New York City official named Robert Moses and his supporters threatened to destroy the beloved gathering place of many New Yorkers. Jane felt she must do something to stop this outrage. Once again she would turn her ideas into action.

Robert Moses had begun his long reign decades earlier, in the 1920s. In addition to running several state offices concerned with parks and roads, he held the positions – often simultaneously – of Commissioner of Parks, City Construction Coordinator, and Slum Clearance Chairman, and he served as the head of other city agencies as well. With the aid of federal funds and the backing of wealthy and powerful leaders, he dreamed of and implemented bold public works ranging from swimming pools and playgrounds to bridges and interstate expressways. Known for both his determination and his arrogance, and never known to avoid conflict, Moses was responsible – more than any other individual – for transforming New York's physical appearance.

Robert Moses (left) and New York Mayor Wagner (right)
visit the Grant Houses construction site, 1956 (see page 49).

Many city officials and much of the general public thought that Moses and his ambitious, large-scale projects had changed New York City for the better. They felt he had brought the city into the modern age by building highways and bridges so that automobile commuters could live in the suburbs and work in the city. He had relocated a huge number of low-income residents from deteriorated buildings to modern public housing projects. He had built parks and developed Jones Beach with restaurants, bath houses, and a boardwalk on Long Island's south shore, and he had masterminded the location of the United Nations headquarters on a seventeen-acre site along the East River. But both his admirers and his critics did agree on one thing: With his enormous power and uncompromising attitude, Moses appeared unstoppable. And he did not mind demolishing anything that stood in his way.

By the 1950s, when Moses was planning a highway through Washington

Square, he had already overseen the construction of several large highways. This required tearing down people's homes and workplaces to make way for speeding automobiles. The residents of these neighborhoods objected, but Moses and his supporters would hear none of it. Moses felt it was more important that the increasing number of cars move quickly through the city, even if close-knit urban communities were sacrificed. It was the price you paid for progress. And the law was on his side. Government officials could take away private property by "eminent domain" if they could show that it benefited the public, and the Federal-Aid Highway Act of 1956 set aside money for a national system of fast roads. Without a highway through Washington Square, Moses argued, traffic in lower Manhattan would grind to a standstill.

Children playing in Washington Square Park, 1950s.
Robert Moses proposed running a four-lane highway through the park.

A once-aspiring actress named Shirley Hayes became an activist mom when she stumbled upon the city's plan to carve up Washington Square Park with a highway. A winding road already extended Fifth Avenue, and buses

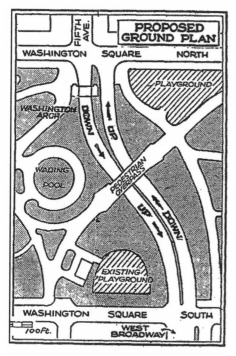

Map of proposed highway through
Washington Square Park, March 11, 1955.

Chess players in Washington Square, 1960s,
at one of many built-in tables.

could turn around at the end of their route in the park. But Shirley discovered the city's plan in 1952 and worked for years to save the park. She organized neighbors to send letters of protest to the mayor and other city officials.

Hoping to save a park where children played and roller-skated and adults chatted or played chess, Jane and her husband Bob joined other dismayed New Yorkers, who barraged city officials with 30,000 postcards. Jane, Shirley, and others set up tables near the park and asked everybody who came by to sign a petition to stop the highway. Many mothers with children in strollers rallied in the park to demonstrate that traffic presented a

60

danger. Older children put up posters and went to protest meetings with their parents. Some children wore sandwich boards with signs front and back informing people about the petitions.

To unite all sorts of neighborhood organizations on this specific issue, the park supporters carefully chose to name their group the Joint Emergency Committee to Close Washington Square to All but Emergency Traffic. A clever strategist, Bob Jacobs convinced their state assemblyman for the West Village district, who was running for re-election, to join other politicians in championing their cause. The new neighborhood-weekly newspaper, the *Village Voice*, promoted the protest in their pages. Even former first lady Eleanor Roosevelt, who had once lived in the Village, lent her support.

Moses was furious when he saw his plan was in danger. At a meeting about the fate of the park, he stood up, gripped the railing, and bellowed, "There is nobody against this – NOBODY, NOBODY, NOBODY, but a bunch of, a bunch of MOTHERS!" Then he stomped out.

To the delight of the Villagers, but not Moses, the Joint Emergency

Washington Square Park, 2007,
with its central fountain, many trees, and sculpted marble arch.

Washington Square Park protest poster
with instructions for sending postcards.

Committee won a thirty-day trial closing of the park to all but fire engines, ambulances, and buses. At a ceremony in November 1958 to celebrate the victory, three-and-a-half-year-old Mary Jacobs and another little girl tied a symbolic traffic-stopping ribbon across the opening of the arch. As the Committee had predicted, no traffic jams occurred and "no drivers begged to come through the park." The following year the city voted to close the park permanently to *all* traffic, and grass eventually grew on the unused roads. The Villagers had succeeded in stopping Moses's plan! And in joining the fight to save Washington Square, Jane had, in her own words, become "a public character" and community leader.

Although she felt compelled to take action to protect her city, it took time away from writing her book. "It's a terrible imposition when the city threatens its citizens in such a way that they can't finish their work," Jane complained. Even her children knew better than to disturb their mother's work, no matter who wished to interrupt. Years later when the mayor of New

York telephoned and asked to speak to Jane, Mary replied firmly, "My mother will not be available for conversation before 4 P.M."

One March evening in 1960 when Jane was tucking eleven-year-old Jimmy into bed, he looked up at her and said sadly, "We're going to lose our tree." The family had planted a tree near the curb in front of their house

Three-and-a-half-year-old Mary Jacobs (center) and another little girl hold the ribbon symbolically closing the park to traffic, November 1, 1958.

several years earlier. "Why do you say that?" his mother asked. Jimmy explained that he had seen men with surveying equipment taking measurements of the sidewalk in front of their house. Ned, who had an interest in surveying, stopped to chat with the men. They told him that the city planned to widen Hudson Street by removing five feet of sidewalk from either side of the street. They would have to cut down the tree.

Like her children, Jane was upset to hear of the city's plans. Hudson Street connected two other busy streets. Robert Moses and his supporters believed that when traffic increased, the solution was to build bigger roads to

Ned and Mary Jacobs manning a petition table
for the Save the Sidewalks campaign on Hudson Street.

accommodate it. But Jane had observed that allowing a greater number of
cars to circulate more easily actually *increased* the amount of traffic. The
next morning the Jacobses wrote a petition to halt the scheme to widen
their street, and they went to the local printer to make copies. At first the
printer told them he was so busy that the job would have to wait a couple of
weeks. But when one of the children exclaimed, "The sidewalks will be cut
off by then!" – the very sidewalk in front of his shop – he listened. The petitions would be ready in an hour.

Telephone lines buzzed, and news of the latest threat spread throughout
Greenwich Village. With the victory in Washington Square Park fresh in
their minds, Villagers from all over the neighborhood formed the Save the
Sidewalks Committee with Jane as the chairman. They placed the petitions

in stores and set up tables along the sidewalk. Ned and Mary Jacobs sat at a table in front of their house and asked passersby to sign the petition because the street widening would be destructive to neighborhood businesses and homes, would be dangerous to children, and would not help reduce traffic.

Because the Save the Sidewalks Committee drew members from the entire district, politicians had to take notice if they wanted to be re-elected. After the Committee delivered the petitions to the Manhattan Borough President's office, the Committee was thrilled to learn that the city had called off the widening of Hudson Street! "Some time after that," Jane later recounted, "Jimmy was on his way home for lunch. He stopped and asked some city workmen who were working on the street what they were doing, and they said, 'We ain't tellin' no little kid nuthin.'"

Looking south on Hudson Street from Charles Street, 1960s.
This neighborhood street might have become a fast and dangerous thoroughfare.

CHAPTER EIGHT

An Attack on City Planning

DESPITE THE distractions of saving Hudson Street and defending Washington Square, Jane managed to use the time afforded by the grant to work on her book. Talks with William Kirk, her own shrewd observations, and many years of writing all came together in the volume she titled *The Death and Life of Great American Cities.*

Jane's opening lines were a battle cry. "This book is an attack on current city planning and rebuilding," she declared. "It is also, and mostly, an attempt to introduce new principles of city planning and rebuilding, different and even opposite from those now taught in everything from schools of architecture and planning to the Sunday supplements and women's magazines."

These schools and magazines merely reflected the popular thinking: Urban renewal was all the rage. Everywhere around the country, cities large and small were enthusiastically tearing down their old districts and proudly rebuilding. Local officials turned to Washington to obtain the federal loans and grants the 1949 Housing Act made available for this purpose.

With her characteristic boldness, Jane challenged not only the idea of urban renewal but also the way architects and city planners decided to rebuild. The Swiss architect Le Corbusier had created one influential scheme called "The Radiant City." In the age of the automobile, he envisioned clusters of tall buildings surrounded by flat grassy spaces, serviced by a network of highways. Many people thought that Le Corbusier's "towers-in-the-park" was an ideal way to provide cities with much-needed housing while preserving open green space.

Photograph of a model
of Le Corbusier's Radiant City proposal for Paris, France, 1935.

But the idea of the Radiant City made no sense to Jane. William Kirk, to whom she expressed her gratitude at the start of her book, had shown her that large-scale projects often destroyed established communities. Without vibrant street life, many of these new projects were bleak and crime ridden – worse than the so-called slums they were supposed to replace. One giant public housing development in St. Louis was such an obvious failure that it had to be abandoned and blown up less than twenty years after it was constructed!

Jane attacked yet another popular planning concept known as the Garden City, where clusters of two- or three-story houses were built around large open greens. Schools, factories, and stores were constructed nearby so that people would not have to travel far to their workplaces as they often did in suburbs. Roads ran around the outside of the housing clusters and connected these island-like communities to one another.

The planned Garden City of Greenbelt, Maryland, 1939. Left center is the community center, school, swimming pool, and shopping center. Houses form rings beyond.

So what was there to dislike about these pleasant places? Too tidy, Jane argued. Like the Radiant Cities, Garden Cities lacked the dense and exciting mix of different people going about their business on bustling streets. Jane saw these all new "cities" as boring places that did not allow for growth and change. She valued wild and unkempt countryside, but she despised orderly suburban "grass, grass, grass."

Many city planners, Jane wrote, were actually anti-city. In their admiration for all that was modern, they wanted to erase the messy old districts that actually *worked*. Instead, they yearned for projects with the dramatic, clean lines of the tall buildings in Le Corbusier's models. Or they supported Garden Cities that drew people away from urban centers. Jane argued that these planners were "interested only in failures" of cities and not curious about what made them successful. *The Death and Life of Great American Cities* made a compelling case for learning from what was in fact working in cities.

Jane believed that the "sidewalk ballet" was impossible if people lived on purely residential blocks. She thought that small businesses, restaurants,

Balducci's on Greenwich Avenue, New York, a fruit and vegetable store
between a florist and a gift shop, open late in the evening, 1960s.

and places of entertainment should be intermingled with housing. She liked
the idea that not far from her home she could find a picture framer, a hair-
dresser, and a store selling diving equipment. She liked having a fish market
near an art gallery. Jane concluded that "mixed uses," a complicated jumble
of activities, were essential for vibrant city life.

Mixed uses also promoted safe city life because they gave people reasons
to be on the sidewalk at all different hours. Residents, shopkeepers, and
pedestrians could serve as "eyes on the street." Jane recounted an incident
that revealed the usefulness of these kindly busybodies. She wrote how, one
day, she watched from her second-floor window as a "struggle" went on
between a man and a little girl. The man seemed to be coaxing the little
girl to follow him. Meanwhile, "the girl was making herself rigid, as children
do when they resist, against the wall of one of the tenements across the
street." Jane was wondering if she should intervene when she saw that she

would not need to. Others had also been watching the struggle.

"From the butcher shop beneath the tenement had emerged the woman who, with her husband, runs the shop; she was standing within earshot of the man, her arms folded and a look of determination on her face." Then, two men came out of a nearby delicatessen. Several more people poked their heads out of windows. Soon, "the locksmith, the fruit man and the laundry proprietor" stepped out onto the street. The man was surrounded. "Nobody," Jane wrote, "was going to allow a little girl to be dragged off even if nobody knew who she was."

As it turned out, the little girl was the man's daughter! Nonetheless, Jane had witnessed a powerful example of the value of "eyes on the street."

Jane went on to reveal another quality of successful city streets. They were composed of short blocks – not the boring super-blocks favored by so many planners. She included diagrams in the book to illustrate her point. Short blocks generated cross streets. More cross streets meant that someone walking from one place to another could choose from many different routes. Besides providing a variation in scenes, these shorter units offered many chances for people to interact because short blocks created lots of street corners.

In *The Death and Life of Great American Cities*, Jane vividly described the kinds of buildings that were needed on these short, lively blocks. It was

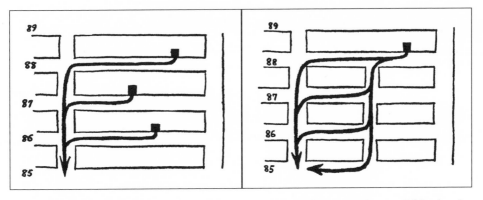

Diagrams from *The Death and Life of Great American Cities* comparing a neighborhood with long blocks to one with short blocks. A person (symbolized by a small square) leaving a house on a long block has only one way to arrive at his destination. A person living on a short block has a choice of routes and, therefore, experiences.

Mixed-age buildings on Christopher Street, Greenwich Village, 2007. The new structure fits between the old.

essential, she insisted, to have a mixture of old and new. With a wide range of buildings, people could afford to buy less expensive, slightly rundown older properties. Buyers could then improve their neighborhood by fixing them up. Jane and Bob had done just that. Furthermore, Jane noted, those who could find different sizes and types of housing within their own neighborhoods were less likely to move away when their needs changed. The area would then become a more stable and desirable place to live.

"New ideas must use old buildings," Jane observed. When an area had inexpensive spaces available, a struggling artist could have a studio, a small ethnic grocery could thrive, or a just-starting skateboard manufacturer could afford to open a business.

Jane was fascinated by the "ingenious adaptations of old quarters to

A new use for an old building – artist Thomas Beale constructed a gallery space to exhibit artwork in this former warehouse building on 11th Avenue near 21st Street, Chelsea, 2007.

new uses. The town-house parlor that becomes a craftsman's showroom, the stable that becomes a house, the basement that becomes an immigrants' club, . . . the warehouse that becomes a factory for Chinese food. . . ."

Stressing the importance of time in the creation of a city, Jane wrote, "Some . . . old buildings, year by year, are replaced by new ones – or rehabilitated. . . . Over the years there is, therefore, constantly a mixture of buildings of many ages and types. This is, of course, a dynamic process, with what was once new in the mixture eventually becoming what is old in the mixture."

But, Jane continued in her sure-handed manner, mixed uses, shorter blocks, and aged buildings were not enough to guarantee a dynamic city. One other element was essential: *people*. Lots of different kinds of people living and working close together. Jane relished life in a densely populated place where people could find others who shared their interests, whether it was studying the mandolin or tasting Indian food. She pointed out that there was a difference between a desirable "high density," where there are many close-together dwellings, and an undesirable overcrowding resulting from too many people within the same dwelling. Planners, she scolded, did not distinguish one from the other.

Some blighted places were true slums with rat-infested housing. But some of the neighborhoods labeled "slums" were, in fact, thriving, healthy communities. In *Death and Life*, Jane praised the North End of Boston and her own Greenwich Village as examples of lively, densely populated districts that were not slums. She had also observed that heavily settled parts of Philadelphia and San Francisco were more appealing places to live in than some of the less populated areas in those same cities.

Too often, Jane railed, people regarded cities as dirty, disease-ridden places. She reminded her readers that remarkable advances in medicine and sanitation now made it possible for large concentrations of people to live together safely. Although disease and pollution were certainly not eliminated, they were no longer major threats. Jane celebrated teeming urban life. She delighted in the many different kinds and nationalities of people who lived in or passed through her neighborhood – from Irish dockworkers

Theater in the street, 16th Street, Chelsea, 1960s.
Temporarily closed to traffic, the street offers neighborhood residents a surprise treat.

to Haitian dancers. She felt she could be a world traveler without going anywhere.

Toward the end of her revolutionary book, Jane insisted that, though many people saw cities as chaotic places, cities have their own underlying order. Jane, who loved to solve jigsaw puzzles, had tried to show her readers that the city was a complex system made of many interlocking pieces. She also contended that urban life was not evil and unnatural, but healthy and orderly.

"Human beings," she wrote, "are, of course, a part of nature, as much so as grizzly bears or bees or whales. . . . The cities of human beings are as natural, being a product of one form of nature, as are the colonies of prairie dogs or the beds of oysters."

Sounding a note of optimism about the future of the great American cities, Jane, the city naturalist, concluded, "Dull, inert cities, it is true, do contain the seeds of their destruction and little else. But lively, diverse, intense cities contain the seeds of their own regeneration. . . ."

Mulberry Street in New York's Chinatown, 2007.
A delightful festival on a Sunday in this dense ethnic urban neighborhood.

CHAPTER NINE

Saving the West Village

WITH HER BOOK finished and awaiting publication, Jane had been back at *Architectural Forum* in February 1961 for only three weeks when her peace was disturbed again. During her routine reading of the newspaper, she came upon a startling item. The city had requested $350,000 from the federal government to study whether her own thriving neighborhood should become a slum clearance project like parts of Harlem or Boston's West End. Fourteen blocks of the West Village – including neighborhood institutions such as the Lion's Head Coffee House and the White Horse Tavern – were facing total demolition. Cities and states had passed laws allowing them to acquire land they deemed blighted, and they could get money from the federal government to help carry out these projects. Jane was shocked. She knew when a city asked Washington for that much money for a "study," they intended to bring in the wrecking ball.

Losing no time, Jane and thirty neighbors rushed to appeal to the Commissioner of Housing and Redevelopment at City Hall. Much to their relief, he granted them a month to prove their neighborhood was not a slum. Experienced at saving a park and at stopping a road-widening project, the Villagers immediately formed the Committee to Save the West Village and chose Jane as the leader. The first meeting drew three hundred people. The group decided to conduct a survey of the neighborhood buildings to prove

The White Horse Tavern on Hudson Street, 2007, a
longtime favorite gathering place for famous writers.

that the West Village was not a slum. Once again, even small children joined
the effort by making posters, distributing leaflets, and running errands.

The Committee's volunteers went door-to-door asking every household
about their living conditions. They documented that virtually all the homes
were well maintained. Many owners had rehabilitated the old but sound properties themselves, preserving the high ceilings, beautiful hand-hewn beams,
and large fireplaces. How could the city think of this as blight and wish to
replace it with an architecturally sterile, high-rise housing development? The
fascination with all things modern blinded many people to old treasures.

Hundreds of people with a variety of jobs – including lawyers, scientists,
artists, shopkeepers, and longshoremen – banded together to save the West
Village. Small groups concentrated on particular tasks such as looking into
legal issues, studying how government works, or translating documents into
Spanish. "Anybody who lived or worked in the neighborhood could belong

Jane with Ned (on stilts) in front of a building
marked with X's to show it should be demolished, 1961.

to the organization," Jane said. "There were no dues and no other qualifications. . . . We never voted on anything. . . . What was done was always what people agreed should be done or at least had no persuasive objection to."

One man who worked inside city government learned – and passed on to the Committee – important information about the laws enabling urban renewal. Only with "citizen participation" could the government carry out a slum clearance project. Telling anyone in state or city government what you wanted for improvements could be cited as citizen participation. Therefore, whenever a government spokesperson asked West Village citizens what they wanted in their neighborhood, the West Villagers knew to reply simply and cleverly, "Drop the slum designation." If the government used this suggestion as citizen participation, there could be no urban renewal project!

The close analysis of typewritten letters, supposedly from different organizations, proved that a variety of documents supporting the urban renewal project were all typed on the same typewriter. Jane presented this evidence at a press conference at the Lion's Head Coffee House.

The Committee members chose to fight the city's plan by raising morale among the group, grabbing attention, and showing they were not intimidated by those in power. They could have fun while working to save their neighborhood, so they often met at the Lion's Head or at Jane's house. She liked to cook and "was a generous feeder of people," said one of her friends.

To attract attention and get publicity from the newspapers, protesters sometimes acted with great fanfare. Waving pennants, they boarded a decorated "sightseeing train" and rode to meetings at City Hall. At one meeting of the City Planning Commission, the chairman, James Felt, declared that city officials were "working closely with the people in the neighborhood." A West Villager responded by producing a loud retching noise. The shocked chairman exclaimed, "I beg your pardon!" but the Villager had clearly made his point, as the audience tried to suppress their laughter.

The urban renewal supporters in the city government fought back by creating what Jane called "puppet organizations" that supported urban renewal. With names like "Neighbors Committee," these organizations sounded as if they were formed by residents but were actually tools for city authorities or builders hoping to profit from new construction.

With a thorough survey that revealed only the slightest amount of blight, Jane and the Committee went to hearings and proved with their evidence that the neighborhood was not a slum. But it made no difference to the city. Refusing to be discouraged, the Committee obtained court orders, organized protest meetings, and packed city hearings with speakers on their behalf. At one city meeting the protesters wore sunglasses with

Protesters from the Village arriving dramatically
at City Hall in a sightseeing train.

City Planning Commission hearing on urban renewal of the West Village, photo in the *New York Times*, June 8, 1961. This hearing at City Hall lasted for more than twelve hours.

large white X's, mimicking the eerie marks on the windows of buildings to be torn down. Jane was the chief spokesperson.

The battle to save the neighborhood raged for months. Apparently aware of the issue's importance to his re-election, New York's Mayor Wagner announced on election eve that he would ask the City Planning Commission to "kill the project." But the next month the Commission overrode the mayor's request. It designated the neighborhood "a blighted area suitable for clearance." With these ominous words ringing in their ears, the Villagers sprang from their seats in what the newspapers called a "near-riot." Despite the Committee's efforts, the city had not budged. Jane summed up what many people believed: "It's the same old story. First the builder picks the property, then he gets the Planning Commission to designate it [as blighted], and then the people get bulldozed out of their homes." As she and the Committee members well knew, many builders and real-estate developers stood to profit handsomely from such urban renewal projects.

"Seven times West Villagers by the hundreds took leave of their jobs and accompanied Mrs. Jacobs to the hearings at City Hall," the Associated Press reported. "The most dramatic of these lasted until 4 A.M. . . . Still it took an appeal to the Mayor to end the battle." Finally on January 31, 1962, after almost a year of fighting to save their neighborhood – and following a strong plea from Mayor Wagner – all the members of the City Planning Commission voted to drop the West Village slum designation. Jane and her collaborators savored this victory but realized their fight was just one of many waiting to be fought in New York and other cities across the country.

Invitation cover, February 1962, possibly by Barbara Ninde Byfield.
The inside of the card reads, "The West Village Neighborhood invites you
to an INDOOR BLOCK PARTY! in Celebration of their Debut
as UNsuitable for Urban Renewal."

Jane dances on the City Hall dome while the community (on the right) runs to City Hall.
A hungry developer (on the left) profits from urban renewal with its cheap emptied land.
The money in the wheelbarrow may be for paying off city officials who have helped him.

CHAPTER TEN

The Impact of *Death and Life*

IN OCTOBER 1961, shortly before the West Village victory, *The Death and Life of Great American Cities* arrived in bookstores. Reviewers across the country immediately hailed Jane's book for its daring originality. From the *San Francisco Chronicle* to the *Wall Street Journal*, critics called it "triumphant," a "major work," and "a path-breaking achievement." Jane's ideas had everyone talking. Large advertisements spread the word. People in government, architects and planners, community groups, and the general public read her eloquent prose. Many were inspired by her provocative views; others disagreed.

Even those who were critical of her work acknowledged the importance of *Death and Life*. A prominent city-planning scholar named Lloyd Rodwin was both Jane's critic and admirer. He began his review in the *New York Times Book Review* by agreeing that recent attempts at urban renewal had failed. He argued, however, that not everyone shared Jane's belief that the best place to live was a densely packed city block. Hadn't many people moved to the suburbs as soon as they could afford to? But Rodwin conceded that "for all its weaknesses," Jane had written a "great book." He proclaimed that "readers will vehemently agree and disagree with the views; but few of them will go through the volume without looking at their streets and neighborhoods a little differently."

Architectural Forum devoted an editorial and a major article to the "clash of ideas" that Jane's work had stirred up. While noting that "FORUM does not agree with everything in Jane Jacobs' book," her editor exclaimed, "Is it not wonderful whenever long-accepted notions in any field are challenged, especially when that challenge is made with high intelligence?" The magazine featured a debate titled "American Cities: Dead or Alive? – Two Views." Criticizing "that book," Boston city planner Edward J. Logue accused Jane of wanting every city to resemble her beloved Greenwich Village. He scoffed at her mistrust of grand plans and declared that "urban renewal is the

Paperback edition, 1961,
published by Vintage/Random House.

most useful tool yet devised to help cities help themselves." Journalist Edward T. Chase disputed this, pointing out that Jane was not against "planning" but against "bad planning." He praised her for helping people view the city as an ecologist might study a delicate and complex natural environment, a system where changes must be made gradually and carefully.

Ad in the *New York Times Book Review:* "They've put up gleaming stone and glass file cabinet housing that breeds delinquency and crime . . . Jane Jacobs says this and much more. . . ."

Despite Chase's words, many city planners felt threatened. "The Jane Jacobs book is going to do a lot of harm, throw a lot of monkey wrenches into the machinery," wrote one planner. "But we are going to have to live with it. So batten down the hatches, boys, we are in for a big blow!" Some planners fought back, scorning the work of an amateur who questioned their expertise. The *Journal of the American Institute of Planners* ridiculed Jane as "The Enchanted Ballerina of Hudson Street." New York's Housing Commissioner Roger Starr mocked what he regarded as Jane's overly romantic vision of the city. In her view, he wrote, "factories nestle beside homes, and never give off smells or smoke" and "streets are thronged day and night, but the traffic is never bothersome or messy." Furthermore, Starr wondered how many people could afford to buy and fix up old houses in Greenwich Village in order to "unslum" the neighborhood. Following Starr

Jane enjoyed and spoke with patrons in a British pub, c. 1962.
Asked to lecture on cities, she traveled throughout the United States and Europe.

as a speaker at a meeting, Jane used him as an example of "how stupid some people can be." Starr retorted dryly, "What a dear, sweet character she isn't."

One of the fiercest attacks on *Death and Life* came from her early supporter, the famous architecture critic Lewis Mumford. In a widely read *New Yorker* magazine article, Mumford sneered at what he called "Mother Jacobs' home remedies." While he shared Jane's harsh attitude towards high-rise urban renewal projects, her attacks on those who, like him, promoted garden cities outraged him. He challenged Jane's assertion that "a city cannot be a work of art." Cities, Mumford thought, should inspire their inhabitants with grand designs and great architecture. Another infuriated man returned Jane's book to its publisher and wrote them a letter. Calling her work "inaccurate," he warned that he could rightfully sue the author for writing things about him that damaged his reputation. "Sell this junk to someone else," he fumed. The letter was signed, "Cordially, Robert Moses."

Despite the assaults on Jane's work, most readers concurred that *The Death and Life of Great American Cities* contained fresh and challenging ideas. As Jane toured the country to promote her book, people sought the

Many cities invited Jane to tour and comment on their plans.
Jane spoke to community groups and officials.

celebrated author's opinions, and she was not shy about offering them. In Pittsburgh, Pennsylvania, Jane praised efforts to make the most of the city's hills and rivers. But she bluntly described their public housing development as "bleak, miserable, and mean." Speaking in West Palm Beach, Florida, Jane admired their waterfront but warned against filling in a cove in order to build a new city auditorium. The plan, she said, would destroy pleasant lakefront views and block cooling breezes. She called the proposed site "disastrous." In Jane's own city, the New York police academy invited her to be a guest lecturer. They valued her insights about sidewalk safety and made *Death and Life* required reading for a police-training course.

Jane's thought-provoking book quickly gained international recognition. A year after its publication in the U. S., her work rolled off presses in the United Kingdom. Before long, readers around the world could buy translations in German, Spanish, Italian, Dutch, Portuguese, Japanese, and Chinese.

CHAPTER ELEVEN

Fighting City Hall and an Expressway

ALTHOUGH MANY readers raved about *Death and Life,* Jane sometimes wondered whether her book could ever help urban planners and city officials see the value of the lively city neighborhoods she described so vividly in her prose. "I would get discouraged about this. I came home once – I'd been on the Lower East Side and I saw the wrecking ball coming down – and went into a grumble and a tirade. I told Bob, 'It doesn't do any good to explain things. It's no use. People are just doing things the same way. It hasn't helped anything.'" Bob, patient and wise, commented thoughtfully, "Now Jane, think how long the Bible has been written and people are still not doing what it says." "Well," Jane thought, "that put it in perspective for me."

Jane had attacked the idea of urban renewal in her book and criticized "expressways that eviscerate great cities," but once again she would have to put her words into action. The highway through Washington Square that Jane had helped stop several years earlier would have served as a ramp leading to an even larger expressway known as the Lower Manhattan Expressway. For decades city officials had considered constructing this giant thoroughfare. Now Robert Moses was determined to carry out the plans.

Instead of going around the outskirts of the city, this ten-lane elevated expressway would cut across the entire width of lower Manhattan, at one point adjacent to the West Village, connecting the Holland Tunnel on the west with the Manhattan and Williamsburg Bridges on the east. On- and off-ramps would extend far into neighborhoods on either side. Running the length of Broome Street, the Lower Manhattan Expressway would destroy large portions of Chinatown, Little Italy, and the mainly Jewish Lower East Side and cast a shadow over whatever remained – all for the sake of drivers hurrying across Manhattan to New Jersey on one side or Long Island on the other.

Wide, fast highways allowed commuters to live in single-family houses, with lawns and trees, far away from their work. Some of these drivers commuted daily to their workplaces in New York from older towns in Westchester County, New York, or in Connecticut. Others came from recently built suburbs with rows of almost identical little box houses, such as those developed by Abraham Levitt and his sons on former farm land, each bearing the name "Levittown" – in New Jersey, Long Island, and Penn-

Aerial view of the newly built suburb of Levittown, Long Island, the first "Levittown," 1947, and a close-up of one of the hundreds of identical homes.

Father La Mountain's church on Broome Street
wedged between storefronts and apartments, 2007.

sylvania. These towns, with hundreds of identical cookie-cutter houses but few stores and little street life, created communities markedly different from the urban mix Jane applauded. "The tolerance, the room for great differences among neighbors," she had written in *Death and Life,* "which are possible and normal in intensely urban life . . . are so foreign to suburbs. . . ."

The colorful communities of Chinatown and Little Italy intermingled at Broome Street and brimmed with mom-and-pop stores and ethnic restaurants. Dozens of architecturally magnificent nineteenth-century commercial buildings with their large expanses of glass between cast-iron columns lined Broome Street. Fearing that demolition could begin at any time, landlords had not kept their buildings in good condition. Artists had moved into the old commercial buildings and lived among the diverse residents and small businesses. But Robert Moses called the cast-iron district (in the area now called Soho) the "most depressed area in lower Manhattan and one of the worst, if not the worst, slums in the entire city."

Building with cast-iron façades on Broome Street that escaped demolition.
These splendid façades now line a main street in the fashionable Soho neighborhood, 2007.

In August 1960, Father Gerard La Mountain became the pastor of the Church of the Most Holy Crucifix on Broome Street. That year, Moses and his allies took advantage of the federal Highway Act of 1956, providing states with ninety percent of all funds to construct interstate highways, and moved ahead with the scheme to run the Lower Manhattan Expressway right through the city. To show their determination, city officials approved a city map with the expressway on it. Father La Mountain knew he had to fight to save his church and the community. In late April 1961 he called a meeting to gather support. People from different religions, opposing political parties, and all sorts of professions attended. Although they normally would not have spoken with one another, they all agreed on a common purpose. They formed the Joint Committee to Stop the Lower Manhattan Expressway.

Father La Mountain had invited Jane, now a well-known author, to the meeting. Although she intended to serve only as a sympathetic observer, she accepted the pastor's request to chair the meeting. "Mrs. Jacobs had a charismatic effect," one newspaper reported. "She began asking questions. What

Architect's drawing of the proposed expressway on Broome Street. Modern buildings with cars below replace the cast-iron district. *Courtesy MTA Bridges and Tunnels Special Archive.*

would happen to the dislocated people? They would be referred, presumably, to antiseptic, anonymous high-rise buildings. . . ." Jane urged people to act and act quickly. In early July, the Board of Estimate, the city's main governing body (including the mayor) responsible for budget and land-use decisions, would hold a hearing at City Hall to decide the fate of the expressway. The Joint Committee to Stop the Lower Manhattan Expressway organized a rally to spread the word and encourage neighborhood residents to attend that hearing. Their work paid off. At the hearing, fifty-nine people gave speeches – fifty-four of them opposed the expressway. Among the speakers were elderly residents of Little Italy and others who had never before spoken in public. Mayor Wagner was overwhelmed and agreed to postpone any decision about the expressway for ninety days. This gave the Committee time to work for their cause.

Throughout the summer the Committee organized more rallies and

Protesters waiting outside New York City Hall,
where most of the official meetings and decisions took place.

obtained more postponements. "They would call a meeting and have three times as many people as they expected and have to find a new hall," recalled community activist Frances Goldin. It showed that the "power of people was greater than the power of cars." Two hundred community groups and politicians of all stripes joined together. "We knew how to form coalitions and get publicity." Arriving on buses from Broome Street, the protesters descended on City Hall and at times lent an atmosphere of theater to the demonstrations. Artists painted signs – some shaped like tombstones – that read: "Little Italy Killed by Progress" or "Death of a Neighborhood" or "People Are More Important Than Cars!" They chanted, "De-map the Broome Street expressway." And Jane and other protesters appeared at one hearing wearing gas masks to draw attention to the pollution the expressway would create.

In December 1962 at a Board of Estimate meeting, local, state, and national political figures praised the proposed ten-lane elevated highway. But the citizens had their say: It would uproot more than 2,000 families and displace 800 small businesses employing 10,000 people. It would destroy a close-knit community and make traffic worse. As part of an interstate highway network, it benefited interstate commuters at the expense of the people of New York. And it was a land-grab plot by powerful real-estate interests who stood to make a lot of money by erecting new buildings on cheap land. At the meeting Jane called Moses's past arguments for a road through Washington

Robert Moses with a model of his proposal for the Brooklyn-Battery Bridge connecting Brooklyn and Manhattan. It was never built.

Square Park "piffle" and said the "same kind of piffle is being put forth by Mr. Moses in support of [the Lower Manhattan Expressway]." After eight hours and forty-four speakers (thirty-nine against the plan), the members of the Board were so exhausted that they postponed their decision another week.

Five days later, the seemingly impossible happened. Mayor Wagner announced that the Board of Estimate had decided to kill the expressway.

People of all ages, interests, and backgrounds joined the
fight to save their homes and neighborhood, 1968.

When the thirty Committee members who had waited at City Hall heard the
news, they hugged and kissed all around. It was an amazing victory! Citizens
had united and succeeded in stopping an interstate highway through the heart
of the country's largest city. The unhappy traffic commissioner accused Jane of
being the person most responsible for stopping the expressway, although she
would never agree. "Thousands of people are responsible for the decision on
Broome Street. If you say I did it, why then other people with a cause will
think that they can't do anything about it without me," Jane told a reporter.

Unfortunately, several years later the Lower Manhattan Expressway
was to raise its ugly head again. "The rule of thumb is that you have to kill
expressways three times before they die," Jane quipped. The plan for the

expressway was revived after John Lindsay became mayor in 1966. He approved a proposal to depress it for part of the route and build housing and schools above. Activists knew what to do and mobilized again.

At the climactic hearing in April 1968, five hundred protesters showed up. More than one hundred were scheduled to speak. According to the pamphlet that the officials handed out for the occasion, the purpose of the hearing was to "give all interested persons an opportunity to be heard concerning their views on the proposed project." But seated together on the stage, the state and city officials, chaired by John Toth of the New York State Department of Transportation, appeared intent on ramming their plan through. They seemed uninterested in hearing serious objections. Because the officials had set up a microphone for the protesters facing away from the stage, the citizens against the expressway felt they addressed only themselves, not the officials on stage with whom they disagreed. Toth allowed his supporters to speak at length, while he limited the amount of time for the

Residents of Little Italy express their feelings about constructing
the Lower Manhattan Expressway through their neighborhood, 1962.

opposition. Protesters carried signs and shouted questions to speakers attempting to sell the expressway proposal, but these speakers chose to ignore them.

Toth made little effort to maintain order. After two hours of bedlam, members of the audience began to call out, "We want Jane. We want Jane." Jane came forward, turned toward the audience, and made a speech suggesting that the entire hearing was a fraud since the officials were going to go ahead with the plan regardless of testimony that evening. Feeling that the protesters had thoroughly and convincingly delivered their message in words, Jane proposed a peaceful march to the podium to demonstrate their point.

Poster for fundraiser to pay Jane's legal bills after her arrest.
Leftover money went to fight against the expressway.

About fifty expressway opponents approached the stage where the officials sat. The frightened stenotypist, who had recorded the proceedings, clutched her machine with one arm and lashed out with the other. The tape fell from her machine to the floor. As they marched by, the protesters stepped on the tape or picked it up and scattered pieces. Seeing the stenotypist's report destroyed, Jane came to a startling realization. "There is no record. There is no hearing. We are through with phony, fink hearings," she told the crowd.

The enraged chairman Toth called for Jane's arrest. Reluctantly and apologetically, the police obliged. Once again chanting "We want Jane," her fellow protesters followed her to the police station. The police released her two hours later, although she would have to hire a lawyer and appear in court on charges of inciting a riot and obstructing government administration. After months of legal hearings, the court ordered Jane to pay a small fine.

But the protesters had made their case. Finally, in August 1969, the Board of Estimate voted unanimously to remove the Lower Manhattan Expressway from the city map. The expressway had now been killed three times, and this time it was truly dead.

CHAPTER TWELVE

Reviving Cities Everywhere

B Y PREVENTING the construction of the Lower Manhattan Expressway, Jane and the Committee showed that when people stood
together and made their voices heard, they could stop the seemingly unstoppable. National newspapers and magazines reported the story
of how these ordinary citizens had prevented a major interstate highway
from going through the middle of a city, a triumph unequaled since public
opposition in San Francisco had halted the Embarcadero Freeway ten
years earlier. News of this recent victory boosted the morale of citizens'
groups around the country. Soon people in New Orleans, Boston, Nash-
ville, and many other cities led "expressway revolts" and convinced their
governments not to slice up their centers with wide fast roads.

The once-outlandish ideas in *Death and Life* and the inspiration of
Jane's actions also helped slow and finally end the massive urban renewal of
aging neighborhoods. Citizens' groups rose up around the country in places
such as Brooklyn's Cobble Hill and Minneapolis's Cedar-Riverside neighborhood, helping to spare these vital old communities from destruction.

People adopted the idea of preserving and rehabilitating old buildings.
In 1965, New York City passed the Landmarks Preservation Law, which pro-
tected certain areas and sites from demolition, and other cities followed suit.
In 1966, the federal government passed the National Historic Preservation

Langham Court, a mixed-income infill housing co-op built in 1991
in Boston's South End National Historic District.

Act, which created the National Register of Historic Landmarks. No building or district listed in the register can be torn down without an extensive review process and justification. Finally in 1974, Congress voted to end the federal urban renewal program originally created by the Housing Act of 1949. Instead, legislation made funds available to local governments to improve and renovate dilapidated neighborhoods as the communities wished.

Gradually the urban planning profession that Jane had attacked came around to her ideas, and architecture schools across the country began teaching urban-planning students to work with citizens to come up with the best plan for their neighborhoods – thus using *real* citizen participation. Cities turned to the concept of "infill" buildings to fill in spaces between existing structures without destroying people's homes. In the West Village, citizens – many of whom had fought hard on the Committee to Save the West Village and now belonged to its successor, the West Village Committee – succeeded in getting government support for and helping to design 475 units of low-rise infill housing in their neighborhood. They placed these moderate-income apartment buildings, called the West Village Houses, in empty lots formerly occupied by an elevated freight railroad.

Cities rehabilitated old districts for new uses. Nearly abandoned waterfronts or industrial sites in such cities as Baltimore and San Francisco were

The popular South Street Seaport, New York, 2007, with its ship museums and shops.
In *Death and Life* Jane advocated the revitalization of New York's old, working waterfront.

converted to popular commercial areas. Other parts of the world responded to Jane's ideas too. Queen Beatrix of the Netherlands valued Jane's brilliant common-sense wisdom and brought her over to consult about ways to build new dense, small-scale housing in Amsterdam.

The obstreperous young girl who trusted her own observations and challenged her teachers had challenged an entire nation to rethink the way cities work – and don't work – and to look at them in a new light. Through her vivid descriptions and logical arguments in *Death and Life*, she had demonstrated the natural way that cities function and the importance of the people who inhabit them and give them life.

Although Jane revealed the value of cities and some basic ingredients of thriving urban life – such as mixed uses and mixed ages of buildings, density, and short blocks – she did not offer a recipe for fixing them. She concluded that every city is a unique and complex system. Jane urged people to look for themselves and cautioned urban planners not to kill what was working. "So if there is any way to follow Jane Jacobs," said the architecture critic Paul Goldberger in 2006, "it is to think of her as showing us not a physical model for city form but rather . . . a model for trusting our eyes and our common sense more than the common wisdom."

With a renewed appreciation of urban life, people today are moving back into city centers. Civic leaders, politicians, and business people have taken a new interest in the central city. Many downtowns in large and small cities all across the United States are spruced up and bustling. Cities, with their concentrated activity, attract new residents and tourists alike. Young

Printer's Row, Chicago. Renovated factory buildings, reflected in the windows, once home to the publishing industry now hold apartments and shops, 2008.

people are flocking to old neighborhoods, such as New York's once doomed, but now revived and trendy Soho.

Jane would be the first to say we shouldn't credit her with all these changes. But her love of cities led millions of people to a new way of seeing and thinking. "Cities [are] the crux of so many different subjects, so many different puzzles," Jane mused. "If you get really interested in them . . . you get in a very shortcut way into so many other subjects. There's almost nothing you can think of that cities don't provide some insight into. So wasn't it lucky to get interested in cities?"

Pike Place Market, Seattle, 2008. In 1969 citizens stopped an urban renewal plan that would have demolished this bustling old market, which first opened in 1907.

Epilogue

IN JUNE OF 1968, Jane Jacobs moved with her family to Canada to prevent her sons from being drafted into the Vietnam War, a war she opposed so strongly that she had ended up in jail as a nonviolent protester.

Jane had barely settled into her new home in Toronto when she learned that here too the city planned to build an expressway that would cut a path through many neighborhoods, including her own. She joined the fight to stop the Spadina Expressway, helping to defeat another major highway and save another city for people instead of cars. Jane denounced the dominance of automobiles and promoted public transportation like subways and buses. In her view, "one great hunk of steel carrying one man is absurd."

Jane and her family lived in an interesting section of Toronto called the Annex – close to downtown and the subway – with bustling main streets and residences ranging from rooming houses to single-family homes. Although she chose to become a Canadian citizen, she stayed in touch with friends and family in the United States. In frequent letters to her mother, who had moved to Virginia near her son John, Jane sent news about the family and garden until Bess Butzner died in 1981 at age 101. In order to remain involved with issues confronting her old neighborhood, Jane subscribed to the West Village Committee newsletter. And she visited New York City from time to time, once in 2004 to speak at a benefit for the low-rise, infill West Village Houses.

In Toronto, when she wasn't growing tomatoes on her roof, traveling to an exotic place, or saving a neighborhood, Jane was writing books, including two works she regarded as her most important. In *The Economy of Cities,* she examined urban settlements throughout history as she considered how cities grow and thrive or stagnate. In *Cities and the Wealth of Nations,* Jane asserted that individual city regions, rather than nations, are the wellsprings of prosperity around the world. Just as she dared to question "expert" city planners, she challenged economists and gained their respect. She also wrote books about ethics, the moral principles governing human behavior. The young girl whose father had taught her the seriousness of promises continued to explore such questions as what happens when virtues like honesty and loyalty come into conflict in the realms of commerce and government.

Jane lived her convictions her entire life. Always energetic, she never ceased to observe, think, and articulate her ideas or participate in a cause in which she believed. After her beloved husband, Bob, died in 1996, Jane continued to live in their house, down the block from her son Jimmy and his family. All three of Jane's children – Jimmy, an inventor and physicist; Ned, a musician and writer; and Burgin, an artist – remained in Canada and had children and grandchildren of their own.

Whitewater rafting in Idaho for five days with a member of Ecotrust and a guide in the summer of 1997 when Jane was 81.

Filming *City Limits*, in which Jane aired her thoughts about cities –
against a backdrop of Toronto sites, 1971.

Throughout the country, Canadian residents and politicians admired
Jane and respected her ideas. In 1998 the Governor General made her a member of the Order of Canada, the country's highest honor, recognizing "a life-
time of outstanding achievement, dedication to the community and service
to the nation." On April 25, 2006, a week before her ninetieth birthday, Jane
died in Toronto. The nation mourned her passing as if she were a head of
state. Canada's television stations and newspapers headlined the sad news
and accompanied it with numerous stories and images of her life and work.

In her later years – although she was never impressed by credentials
and turned down all honorary degrees – Jane had received many awards.
After her death, in 2007, the Rockefeller Foundation established the Jane
Jacobs Medal to recognize people who put "Jacobsonian principles and
practices in action in New York City." But the grant it had awarded to Jane
in 1958 to write a book about cities may have been the best award of all.

Since its publication, *The Death and Life of Great American Cities* has
been translated into dozens of languages and sold millions of copies.
Although it never appeared on a "bestseller" list, it has kept on selling steadily
in the U.S. and Canada and around the world. It has remained in print continuously since it first shook the world in 1961.

Chronology of Jane's Life

1916	May 4. Birth of Jane Isabel Butzner in Scranton, Pennsylvania
1933	Graduates from Central High School, Scranton
1934	Works as assistant to women's-page editor at *Scranton Tribune*
1934	Moves in with sister in Brooklyn
1935	Moves with sister to 55 Morton Street in Greenwich Village
1935	*New York Herald Tribune* publishes poem
1935	Sale of first story – to *Vogue* magazine
1937	Father dies at age 59
1938	Begins classes at the University Extension at Columbia University
1940	Publishes article in *Cue* magazine on manhole covers
1940	Begins work for *The Iron Age* magazine
1943	Gets job as feature writer for the U.S. Office of War Information
1944	Marries Robert Hyde Jacobs Jr. while living at 82 Washington Place
1945	Gets work as a reporter for the U.S. State Department
1947	Buys former candy store at 555 Hudson Street and renovates it as home
1948	Birth of son James Kedzie (Jimmy) Jacobs
1950	Birth of son Edward Decker (Ned) Jacobs
1952	Starts job as associate editor at *Architectural Forum*
1955	Birth of daughter, Mary Hyde (later called Burgin) Jacobs
1955	Receives tour of East Harlem from William Kirk
1956	Speaks on urban renewal at Harvard University
1958	Washington Square is closed to traffic
1958	Publishes "Downtown Is for People" in *Fortune* magazine
1958	Receives grant from the Rockefeller Foundation
1958	Takes leave from *Architectural Forum* to write book
1960	Fights to Save the Sidewalks along Hudson Street in the West Village
1961	Begins fight to Save the West Village
1961	Publication of *The Death and Life of Great American Cities*
1962	Joins fight to stop the Lower Manhattan Expressway
1967	Arrested in anti-Vietnam War protest
1968	Arrested for Lower Manhattan Expressway protest

1968   Moves with family to Toronto to keep sons from the Vietnam War

1974   Becomes a Canadian citizen

1981   Mother, keeper of scrapbooks of news clippings about Jane, dies at 101

1988   Receives the Encyclopædia Britannica Award for the Dissemination of Learning and the Enrichment of Life

1996   Husband, Robert Hyde Jacobs Jr., dies

1997   Toronto sponsors conference called "Jane Jacobs and Ideas That Matter"

1998   Named to the Order of Canada, the nation's highest honor

2000   Awarded the National Building Museum's Vincent Scully Prize in Washington, D.C.

2004   Receives the Couchiching Award for Public Policy Leadership in Canada

2006   April 25. Jane Jacobs dies in Toronto

2007   Rockefeller Foundation establishes the Jane Jacobs Medal

2007   May 4. Toronto declares Jane Jacobs Day

Books by Jane Jacobs

United States. Constitutional Convention (1787). Constitutional Chaff: Rejected Suggestions of the Constitutional Convention of 1787 with Explanatory Argument. Compiled by Jane Butzner [Jacobs]. New York: Columbia University Press, 1941.

The Death and Life of Great American Cities. New York: Random House, 1961.

The Economy of Cities. New York: Random House, 1969.

The Question of Separatism. New York: Random House, 1980.

Cities and the Wealth of Nations. New York: Random House, 1984.

The Girl on the Hat. Toronto: Oxford University Press, 1989. (A picture book for children with illustrations by Karen Reczuch)

Systems of Survival. New York: Random House, 1992.

A Schoolteacher in Old Alaska: The Story of Hannah Breece. New York: Random House, 1995.

The Nature of Economies. New York: Random House, 2000.

Dark Age Ahead. New York: Random House, 2004.

Notes

The following notes explain where we found quotations and the most important or little-known pieces of information.

CHAPTER ONE: An Obstreperous Young Girl

In a letter found in the Jane Jacobs Papers at Boston College (BC) and also published in *Ideas That Matter* (ITM), p. 3, Jane wrote that after second grade she "mostly taught myself" by reading books in her lap. The story about Jane refuting that cities grow up around waterfalls comes from ITM, p. 26.

CHAPTER TWO: Growing Up in the Electric City

We found information about Jane's ancestors and details of her life in Alexiou's biography of Jane, *Urban Visionary* (Alexiou), and in Jane's introduction to her recipe in *At Grandmother's Table*. We also used an article about Bess Butzner in *The Scrantonian* on June 15, 1969, Jane's interview with Jim Kunstler (Kunstler), and documents in ITM. Information about Scranton comes from the Lackawanna Historical Society, Scranton city directories at the Albright Memorial Library in Scranton, and *Scranton*, a highly illustrated history of the city. The stories of and quotes about Jane's school antics are from ITM, pp. 16–17. Jane's description of the streetcars is from her book *The Economy of Cities*. The letter from Thomas Lomax Hunter is at BC. Jane spoke of her first visit to New York in her Kunstler interview. Information about Scranton in the Depression comes from the Lackawanna Historical Society. "Eager to get a job. . . ." is from ITM, p. 3. Quotes about her Appalachian experience are from Jane's *Dark Age Ahead*.

CHAPTER THREE: Becoming a Writer in New York

Jane spoke of her early days in New York with Kunstler. Also see ITM, pp. 35–36 and Alexiou. "While Arranging Verses for a Book" is at BC. Quotes about manhole covers appeared in her *Cue* magazine article, May 1940. She spoke of her imaginary conversations in an interview with Robert Fulford in *Azure* magazine in 1997 (Fulford). Jane wrote of her Columbia experience in a letter at BC, also ITM, p. 4. Peter Laurence in his article "Jane Jacobs Before *Death and Life*" (Laurence) describes *Constitutional Chaff* (the entire manuscript can be found online). For the *Scrantonian's* article praising Jane's efforts to help Scranton, see ITM p. 37 and BC. The "Look What Happened" flier, Jane's "Daily's Effort Saves City From 'Ghost Town' Fate" in *Editor and Publisher*, and an account of Jane's union activities in an unknown and undated newspaper headlined, "Chilton Boss Says He Won't Do It Again" are all at BC.

CHAPTER FOUR: Cupid and the Candy-Store House

Information about *Amerika Illustrated* is from Laurence. The cupid quote is from the Fulford interview. Jane and Bob's wedding details can be found in ITM, p. 37. John Simon, a former editor at Random House, provided the recollection about the house he later occupied. The quotes about Hudson Street are from ITM, p. 49 and 52. Jane's description and all the quoted material about the "sidewalk ballet" come from *The Death and Life of Great American Cities* (*Death and Life*), chapter 2.

CHAPTER FIVE: Reporting and Learning at *Architectural Forum*

Laurence provided a summary of Jane's career at *Architectural Forum*, and urban historian Alexander von Hoffman explained American cities in crisis. Jane's story of her Philadelphia trip appeared in Alexiou and *The Villager*, May 12–18, 2004. She wrote of her admiration for Boston's North End in *Death and Life*, chapter 16 and others. For Jane's meeting with William Kirk, her tours of East Harlem, and her work on the Union Settlement Board, see Alexiou, pp. 43–49. *In These Times*, July 25, 2006, noted Jane's efforts to involve East Harlem residents in housing design.

CHAPTER SIX: Jane's Good *Fortune* Article

We found the story of Jane's stage fright and talk at Harvard in ITM, pp. 16–17. The text of Jane's talk appeared in *Architectural Forum*, June 1956. Jane's *Fortune* magazine article "Downtown Is for People," April 1958, can be found in *The Exploding Metropolis*. Laurence gave details about Jane's Rockefeller Foundation grant. For an account of Jason Epstein's editorial career, see Alexiou, pp. 64–65.

CHAPTER SEVEN: A Bunch of Mothers . . . and Children

The story of the fight to save Washington Square was pieced together from many articles in the *New York Times*, Laurence's article, and Robert Fishman's chapter "The Revolt of the Urbs" in *Robert Moses and the Modern City*. This book also provided much of the information on Robert Moses. The "bunch of mothers" quote is from the Kunstler interview. For the story of the mayor's phone call, see ITM, p. 22. The Save the Sidewalks tale is from *The Villager,* March 20, 1960, and ITM, pp. 67 and 71.

CHAPTER EIGHT: An Attack on City Planning

All quotations in this chapter are from *Death and Life.* "This book is an attack. . ." are the opening lines of chapter 1. Also in this chapter are Jane's views on the Radiant City, the Garden City, and her distaste for grass. For a description of "mixed uses," see chapter 8. "Eyes on the street" and the story of the man and the little girl appear in chapter 2. Jane's argument for short blocks comes from chapter 9. She considered new ideas, older buildings, and the importance of time in the creation of a city in chapter 10, and high density versus overcrowding in chapter 11. Discussions of disease in cities are found in chapters 11 and 22. The idea that a city dweller could feel like a world traveler comes from chapter 12. Jane described cities as natural systems capable of regeneration in chapter 22.

CHAPTER NINE: Saving the West Village

ITM, p. 49, and numerous articles from the *New York Times* and the *Village Voice* offered details of the neighborhood struggle. In the World Bank Group's interview, Jane described the continuing West Village Committee and said, "Anybody who lived or worked. . . ." The "drop the slum designation" story appeared in Alexiou, p. 106. Max Allen called Jane "a generous feeder. . . ." "It's the same old story. . . ." comes from the *New York Times,* October 19, 1961, and "kill the project" from the same paper on February 1, 1962. "Seven times West Villagers. . . ." is from an undated clipping at BC.

CHAPTER TEN: The Impact of *Death and Life*

We found a good collection of reviews of *Death and Life* at BC. For Lloyd Rodwin's review, see the *New York Times Book Review,* November 5, 1961. The *Architectural Forum* editorial about *Death and Life* appeared in their January 1962 issue, and the debate between Logue and Chase in their March 1962 issue. The advice to "batten down the hatches" appears in an article from the *American Society of Planning Officials Newsletter,* February 1962, and in ITM, p. 10. A reviewer in the *Journal of the American Institute of Planners* ridiculed Jane as "The Enchanted

Ballerina of Hudson Street," May 1962. Roger Starr's comments can be found in ITM, pp. 15 and 53. For Lewis Mumford's swipe at "Mother Jacobs," see the *New Yorker*, December 1, 1962. The letter from Robert Moses to Bennett Cerf resides at BC. For an account of Jane's visits to Pittsburgh and West Palm Beach, see the *Pittsburgh Post-Gazette*, February 20, 1962, and the *Miami Herald*, March 18, 1962, both at BC. Jane's invitation from the New York Academy of Police Science is also at BC.

CHAPTER ELEVEN: Fighting City Hall and an Expressway

The opening anecdote and Bob's wise words can be found in ITM, p. 16. "Expressways that eviscerate great cities" is from *Death and Life*, chapter 1. The Levittown Historical Society provided facts about Levittown. "The tolerance, the room for differences. . . ." is from *Death and Life*, chapter 3. Much information about the fight was reported in the *New York Times*, the *Village Voice*, and the *Washington Post*, and other material came from *New York* magazine and Disk 7 of Ric Burns's video series *New York: A Documentary Film*. Robert Moses's words "most depressed area. . . ." appeared in this video as did the quotes from Frances Goldin, "They would call a meeting. . . ." "Mrs. Jacobs had a charismatic effect. . . ." was in the *National Observer*, December 24, 1962. The "same kind of piffle. . . ." was quoted in the *Village Voice*, December 13, 1962. Jane's words "thousands of people are responsible. . . ." appeared in the same paper on December 12, 1962. "The rule of thumb. . . ." is in Alexiou, p. 111. Jane tells the story of the climactic April 1968 expressway hearing in a long statement in ITM, pp. 74–78. The *Village Voice's* account is printed in ITM, p. 73. We found the outcome of Jane's arrest in Christopher Klemek's article in the January 2008 issue of the *Journal of Urban History*.

CHAPTER TWELVE: Reviving Cities Everywhere

Expressway revolts are listed in a *Washington Post* article, "Freeway Building Was Once Simple," August 31, 1969. Ned Jacobs mentioned his mother's influence on the people of Cobble Hill in the *Alternatives Journal*, June 2002, and we learned of the successful neighborhood revolt in Minneapolis in *Revitalizing Urban Neighborhoods*, edited by W. Dennis Keating et al. The Municipal Art Society's exhibition on Jane Jacobs (September 2007–January 2008) provided information about the West Village Houses. Material about Jane and Queen Beatrix is at BC. Paul Goldberger's words come from *Block By Block: Jane Jacobs and the Future of New York*. We read Jane's musing that "Cities are the crux. . . ." in Mark Feeney's interview in ITM, p. 13.

EPILOGUE

Jane stated that "one great hunk of steel carrying one man is absurd" in the film *City Limits*. She mentioned her subscription to the West Village Committee newsletter in her interview with the World Bank Group. *The Villager*, May 5–May 18, 2004, describes her speech at the West Village Houses benefit. Information about Jane's children and grandchildren and the Order of Canada award appeared in the *Globe and Mail* obituary of Jane. Random House verified information about the sales and translations of *The Death and Life of Great American Cities*.

Selected Bibliography

Our interest in Jane Jacobs was sparked long ago when we read *The Death and Life of Great American Cities*. Aiming to introduce her work to young people, we began by searching the Internet for sources. We discovered that Jane had given her papers to the John J. Burns Library at Boston College, a most convenient coincidence for two Boston-area residents. Jane's papers provided us a treasure trove of articles, letters (including a note from Jane to her mother explaining why she had been jailed yet again), photos, and extensive scrapbooks of news clippings assembled by her mother. Max Allen selected and published many of the best of these primary documents and photos in *Ideas That Matter: The Worlds of Jane Jacobs*, creating what he called a "biography-without-a-biographer." This book became an invaluable guide and source for us.

As much as possible, we looked to Jane's own words in her writings, lectures, interviews, and two films in which she appeared. Secondary sources lent additional information and helped with detective work. For example, we read about but could not find Jane's *Cue* magazine piece about manhole covers. A footnote in Peter Laurence's scholarly article in the *Journal of the Society of Architectural Historians* about Jane's early years revealed the date of the issue. Harvard University's Widener Library held this New York arts guide from 1940, and we finally laid our hands on "Caution · Men Working."

As artists and illustrators, we value the communication of pictures and tried to locate elucidating images. The hunt for historic photos proved at least as challenging as sleuthing for facts. In addition to combing the photo archives at the Library of Congress or various newspapers, we literally stumbled upon Ned Otter in Washington Square Park selling his photographer father's stunning 1960s images.

And, as Jane urged, nothing can replace looking with your own eyes. Visiting Scranton and getting a sense even today of what this American gritty city had been more than three-quarters of a century earlier was truly indispensable.

Here are some of our sources that may be of interest in finding out more about Jane and her world.

BOOKS ABOUT OR ON TOPICS RELATED TO JANE JACOBS

Allen, Max, ed. *Ideas That Matter: The Worlds of Jane Jacobs*. Ontario, Canada: The Ginger Press, 1997. A collection of primary sources by and about Jane. Photos.

Alexiou, Alice Sparberg. *Jane Jacobs: Urban Visionary*. New Brunswick, New Jersey: Rutgers University Press, 2006. The only adult biography of Jane. Her life, work, and activism, including the latter half of her life in Canada and her later books as well.

Ballon, Hillary and Kenneth T. Jackson, eds. *Robert Moses and the Modern City: The Transformation of New York*. New York: W. W. Norton, 2007. An exhibition catalogue with scholarly articles evaluating Moses. Many photos of his projects.

Berkeley, Ellen Perry. *At Grandmother's Table*. Minneapolis: Fairview Press, 2000. Recipes handed down from grandmothers to granddaughters and reminiscences by the latter, including Jane Jacobs.

The Editors of *Fortune. The Exploding Metropolis*. Garden City: New York, 1958. Contains Jane's ground-breaking *Fortune* magazine article, "Downtown is for People."

Kashuba, Cheryl A., Darlene Miller-Lanning and Alan Sweeney. *Scranton* (Images of America series). Charleston, South Carolina: Arcadia Publishing, 2005. Scranton's history portrayed largely in illuminating historic photos from the Lackawanna Historic Society.

Mennel, Timothy, Jo Steffens and Christopher Klemek, eds. *Block By Block: Jane Jacobs and the Future of New York*. Municipal Art Society of New York: Princeton

Architectural Press, 2007. A companion publication to the Municipal Art Society's exhibition, containing more than forty short essays in response to Jane's work.

Stonehill, Judith. *Greenwich Village: A Guide to America's Legendary Left Bank.* New York: Universe, 2002. A lovely, illustrated, pocket-size introduction.

Interviews with Jane Jacobs (Web address, if online)

Feeney, Mark. "City Sage," *Boston Globe*, November 14, 1993. (Also in ITM p. 10–13)

Harris, Blake. "Cities and Web Economies: Interview with Jane Jacobs," *New Colonist*, 2002. (http://www.newcolonist.com/jane_jacobs.html)

Kunstler, James Howard (Jim). Interview with Jane Jacobs on September 6, 2000, *Metropolis Magazine*, March 2001. (www.kunstler.com/mags_jacobs1.htm)

Rochon, Lisa. "Jane Jacobs at 81," *Metropolis Magazine*, April 1998. (http://www.metropolismag.com/html/content_0498/ap98jane.htm)

Steigerwald, Bill. "City Views," *Reason*, June 2001. (http://www.reason.com/news/show/28053.htm)

The World Bank Group, "Urban Economy and Development," Interview of Jane Jacobs with Roberto Chavez, Tia Duer, and Ke Fang, Toronto, February 4, 2002. (www.worldbank.org/urban/forum2002/docs/jj-full.pdf)

Magazine Articles (Web address, if online)

Blake, Peter. "About Mayor Lindsay, Jane Jacobs and James Bogardus," *New York*, May 6, 1968.

Butzner, Jane [Jacobs]. "Caution · Men Working," *Cue*, May 18, 1940.

Fulford, Robert. "Radical Dreamer: Jane Jacobs on the Streets of Toronto," *Azure Magazine*, October–November, 1997. (http://www.robertfulford.com/jacobs.html)

Goldberger, Paul. "Uncommon Sense," *American Scholar*, Autumn 2006. (http://www.theamericanscholar.org/uncommon-sense)

Gopnik, Adam. "Cities and Songs," *New Yorker*, May 17, 2004. (http://www.newyorker.com/archive/2004/05/17/040517ta_talk_gopnik)

Jacobs, Ned. "Changing the World by Saving Place," *Alternatives Journal*, June 2002. (http://www.accessmylibrary.com/coms2/summary_0286-25695254_ITM)

Klemek, Christopher. "From Political Outsider to Power Broker in Two 'Great American Cities,'" *Journal of Urban History*, January 2008.

Laurence, Peter L. "Jane Jacobs Before *Death and Life,*" *Journal of the Society of Architectural Historians,* March 2007. (http://www.bwaf.org/images/pdf/Laurence-Jacobs_JSAH.pdf)

Mumford, Lewis. "Mother Jacobs' Home Remedies," *New Yorker*, Dec. 1, 1962.

Zipp, Sandy, "Jane Jacobs, Reconsidered," *In These Times,* July 25, 2006. (http://www.inthesetimes.com/article/2743)

NEWSPAPER ARTICLES

In the *New York Times,* the *Washington Post* (both available online through some libraries), and the *Village Voice* (available on microfilm in some libraries), you can read many articles about the battles in which Jane was involved.

Amateau, Albert. "Jane Jacobs Comes Back to the Village She Saved," *The Villager,* May 5–May 18, 2004. (http://www.thevillager.com/villager_54/janejacobs.html)

Atkinson, Brooks. "Critic at Large: Jane Jacobs, Author of Book on Cities, Makes the Most of Living in One," *New York Times*, December 10, 1961.

"Bess Butzner, Ex-Teacher-Nurse, Celebrates 90th Birthday Saturday," *The Scrantonian*, June 15, 1969.

Feeney, Mark. Jane Jacobs obituary, *Boston Globe*, April 26, 2006.

Martin, Douglas. Jane Jacobs obituary, *New York Times*, April 26, 2006.

Martin, Sandra. Jane Jacobs obituary, *Globe and Mail* (Toronto), April 26, 2006.

Rodwin, Lloyd. "Neighbors Are Needed" (Review of *The Death and Life of Great American Cities*), *New York Times Book Review,* November 5, 1961.

FILMS AND VIDEOS

Burns, Ric. *New York: A Documentary Film*, Disk 7. 1999. This episode of the city's history shows how the powerful Robert Moses shaped the city – for better or worse. Includes an account of Jane's role in protests against the Lower Manhattan Expressway and passages from *The Death and Life of Great American Cities.*

Hyde, Laurence. *City Limits*. National Film Board of Canada, 1971. Jane appears in this film and talks about cities, using Toronto as an example.

Picture Credits

All photos depict New York City unless the caption reads otherwise.

The photographs in this book are from the following sources and are used by permission and through the courtesy of the copyright owners:

Pages 3 [Reproduction number: LC-USZ62-137839], 58 [LC-USZ62-137834], 59 [LC-USZ62-137836], 69 [LC-USF344-007788-ZB], 80 [LC-USZ62-137838], 81 [LC-USZ62-137837], 96 [LC-USZ62-137835], 97 [LC-USZ62-136079] Library of Congress, Prints and Photographs Division

Pages 14, 16, 20 (right), 37, 38, 44, 63, 64, 79, 110 From *Ideas That Matter*, with the permission of Max Allen

Pages 15, 30, 32 From the collection of the Lackawanna Historical Society

Pages 17, 25, 26, 39, 40–41, 55, 61, 72, 73, 75, 78, 93, 94, 104 Photos by Glenna Lang

Pages 18, 19 Brown Brothers, Sterling, Pennsylvania

Pages 20 (left), 31, 83, 89, 100, 108, 111 From the Jane Jacobs Archive, John J. Burns Library, Boston College, with the permission of the Trustees of Boston College

Page 24 *People Mostly: New York in Photographs, 1900–1950*, by Benjamin Blom

Pages 27, 28, 60 (right), 65, 70, 74 Photos by Robert Otter © 2008 Ned Otter

Page 29 "View of Low Library," with the permission of the University Archives, Columbia University in the City of New York

Page 36 *Amerika Illustrated*, No. 43, 1950

Page 45, 48, 49 Photographs and Prints Division, Schomburg Center for Research in Black Culture, The New York Public Library, Astor, Lenox and Tilden Foundations

Page 46, 68 Courtesy of the Frances Loeb Library, Harvard Graduate School of Design

Page 47 Photo by Nishan Bichajian, Courtesy of Kepes/Lynch Collection, Rotch Visual Collections, Massachusetts Institute of Technology

Page 52 Photo by Bob Gomel/Time Life Pictures/Getty Images

Pages 53, 54, 105, 106 Photos by Marjory Wunsch

Page 60 (left), 82 *New York Times,* March 11, 1955, and June 8, 1961

Page 62 Collection of the New-York Historical Society. [Negative #80479d]

Page 68 © 2008 Artists Rights Society (ARS), New York/ADAGP, Paris/FLC

Page 71, 86, 87 From *The Death and Life of Great American Cities* by Jane Jacobs,

Acknowledgments

We are grateful to all who helped in archives and obtaining photographs: Mary Ann Moran-Savakinus and Robert Booth at the Lackawanna Historical Society; Ann Glorioso at the Levittown Library; Barbara Natanson and Marilyn Ibach at the Prints & Photographs Division, Library of Congress; Jo Steffens at the Municipal Art Society; Miranda Schwartz and Itty Mathew at the New-York Historical Society; Mary Daniels and Alix Riskind at Harvard's Loeb Library; Justine Hyland and David Horn at Boston College's Burns Library; Elizabeth Phipps at MIT's Rotch Library; Carol Butler at Brown Brothers; Laura Rosen at MTA Bridges and Tunnels Special Archive; Allison Scola, Robert Ast, and Jocelyn K. Wilk at Columbia University; Melissa Baldock at the Greenwich Village Society for Historic Preservation; Judi Keller at the Albright Memorial Library in Scranton; Virginia Goodrich and Austin Burke at the Greater Scranton Chamber of Commerce; Ned Otter; and Gloria McDarrah.

Thanks to Max Allen, Erik Wensberg, John Simon, and Judith Stonehill for first-hand stories about Jane; to Robert Fishman, Peter Laurence, Christopher Klemek, Jay Wickersham, and Norman Glickman for advice and information; to Mark Frudd for superb photo retouching; to Thomas Beale and Mickey Western for the photo op; to James M. Shea at the Longfellow National Historic Site and Leonard McGee for photo reference materials; to Susan Monsky and Mark Hirsch for so much.

Thanks to James Wunsch for suggesting that young people should know about Jane Jacobs; and to urban historian Alexander von Hoffman for his indispensable tutelage and expertise about the spirit and issues of the times that Jane lived in. Thanks to David R. Godine for believing in this book and guiding it so thoughtfully; and to Carl W. Scarbrough, Sue Ramin, and the team at Godine for all their assistance.

Index

Page numbers followed by an asterisk [*] indicate illustrations.

About the Authors

Glenna Lang's previous work includes illustrations for classic poems for children with Godine: Robert Louis Stevenson's *My Shadow*, James Whitcomb Riley's *When the Frost Is on the Punkin*, Henry Wadsworth Longfellow's *The Children's Hour*, and Robert Frost's *The Runaway*. She wrote and illustrated *Looking Out for Sarah*, winner of the American Library Association's Schneider Family Award. Although she grew up in New York City, she has lived for many years with her husband, Alexander von Hoffman, in Cambridge, Massachusetts, and teaches at the School of the Museum of Fine Arts, Boston. They often visit their daughter, Esmé, in her fifth-floor walk-up apartment in an old building in Soho.

Marjory Wunsch has illustrated numerous children's books, including *The Answered Prayer, Junkyard Dog,* and *Never Take a Pig to a Party*. She is author and illustrator of *Spaceship Number Four* and *Aunt Belle's Beach*. Her artwork has also appeared in *Dr. Bowdler's Legacy* for David Godine and in publications such as the *Boston Globe, Harvard Magazine,* and the *New York Times Book Review*. While studying architecture at Harvard's Graduate School of Design in the early 1970s, she encountered problems of urban design, rehabilitation of old buildings, and the ideas of Jane Jacobs. Marjory and her husband, Carl Wunsch, live in Cambridge, Massachusetts. They have two grown children and a grandchild.